Creative Christian Media

Secrets of Successful Media Ministry

—◦◦◦—

By
Phil Cooke, Ph.D.

Compiled & Edited by
Bob Keith Bonebrake

xulon
PRESS

Preface

—ɱ—

This book is the result of ten years of writing for numerous magazines, both religious and secular, dealing with the needs and questions of Christian broadcasters. My editor, Bob Bonebrake and I have combined many articles, updated others, and organized this book into six major categories, corresponding to some of the most frequent questions I have received about the Christian media. These questions include:

1) What is the future of Christian media?
2) When and how should I change my media ministry to respond to changing times?
3) How should I select, manage and train my people?
4) How can I find creative content for my media ministry?
5) How can I stay ahead of technology changes?
6) How can I better understand my audience?

In addition, I've provided an appendix to deal with specific areas of Christian media that are especially challenging to producers. It is my hope that these appendix articles will provide continuing help for pastors, ministry leaders, and their media team.

As a television producer in Hollywood – particularly one who spends time helping churches and ministries improve and expand their media outreach – I'm often asked why so many ministries are drawn to the media. After all, it's very expensive. Could we better use that money for feeding the hungry, or helping the homeless? Is it a waste to spend millions of dollars on television and radio? Would we be better stewards of God's money if we spent that money on more traditional evangelism?

All good questions. Today finances are tight for many churches and ministries. No one wants to waste precious resources needed to reach this modern culture that we have been called to transform.

My first response is to study the life of Jesus. How and where did He reach people? How did He make an impact? What lessons can we learn from His ministry?

The fact is Jesus knew where the people were, and He spent his time reaching them. He could be found in the marketplace, the temple square, at social gatherings, and in the places where people debate and discuss ideas. Two thousand years later, our equivalent of those places is the media – radio, television, movies, and the Internet. Research indicates that most people spend up to four hours each day watching TV and surfing the web. Every major advertiser in America knows that if you want to reach the largest potential audience, the media is the marketplace of the 21st century.

That's why I've spent my career in the media. When I was a kid growing up during the 50s and 60s, my church was involved in door-to-door evangelism, walking from house to house personally sharing the gospel with anyone who would come to the door. But today, that's nearly impossible. Personal evangelism is still important, but when a stranger shows up at a doorstep today, he or she is usually considered a nut or a threat – especially in a culture where crime and security issues are so prevalent. That's why it can be more effective to reach into every home through the media.

The sheer numbers we can reach through the media make technology an essential part of today's evangelism. Every day throughout the world, hundreds of millions of people are watching TV, listening to the radio, reading magazines, or using the Internet. The entertainment industry understands the power of those numbers, and spends billions of dollars to reach this vast audience.

How can we miss this opportunity for the cause of Christ? You may love the media or hate it, but the fact is, the media reaches a potential audience numbering in the billions globally. Reaching this audience for Christ has the potential to shake nations of the world.

Why we use the media was settled long ago. The question now is how can we use the media most effectively? A typical local church can reach thousands of people in its city, but through the media, that same church can reach millions around the world.

Jesus spent his life reaching people. Today, we use new tools to do the same thing. I would encourage you to be part of this remarkable moment in time, touching nations through the power of the media.

Introduction

The New Media World

—ᴍ—

Television has been called a vast wasteland. It's hard to argue with that description. Even today, with multiple cable and satellite channels, Christian and family channels, and other positive signs, there are still barren deserts out there on the media landscape.

But recently, the mass media has changed in a way no one expected. In fact, I predict our time will be remembered as the death of mass media. In truth, the media is being murdered. The suspects include digital music and video players, broadband Internet connections, blogs, and online entertainment.

There will be no survivors.

Today, media is about personalization. The "mass audience" isn't interested in the same old things anymore. The audience wants its media customized.

As of this writing, eBay has 168 million users worldwide, MySpace.com has 40 million users, there are 23 million blogs and 10 million people use CraigsList to search for classified ads.

What's the connection?

Each of these web-related media can be customized for the individual. On my iPod, I have classic rock and roll music, bluegrass, praise and worship, Frank Sinatra, southern gospel, and even opera. I'm not interested in what radio stations think I want to hear – now I customize my own playlist.

What does this mean for Christians interested in sharing their faith?

It means it's time Christians wake up to change.

This book is about being ready for that change, and being willing to step into the future.

Christian broadcasters always thought they had the answer to what the audience wanted. They assumed they knew how to make the audience listen. But today, the audience is in transition. In a 500-cable channel universe, the audience has more choices than ever before, and for us to justify their attention, we need to get on their wavelength. After all, it doesn't matter if you have a great message if no one is listening.

There are some media ministries that "get it," but most have no clue. What exactly do the successful ones know? Here are a few important keys to being a successful media minister:

1) Be yourself. Don't try to be the next Billy Graham, Joyce Meyer, T.D. Jakes, or Joel Osteen. God has called you to a unique calling and purpose. Every week I get calls from pastors and ministry leaders wanting me to do the same thing for them that I've done for big, well-known media clients. There are a lot of copy cats out there, but that's the last thing the world needs. The culture isn't looking for a copy of an existing famous leader, they're looking for you. If you have a calling to reach the world - the world is waiting.

2) Be honest. Let's face it. Not every book and teaching tape you produce is going to transform lives, change the culture, or shake up nations. The cry of this generation is authenticity. We make a lot of promises when it comes to promoting products on TV. Be proud of what you do, and pitch your products and projects with passion, but also be real. That's what makes the audience respond.

3) Understand the power of ideas. Most churches and ministries pay enormous amounts of money for media airtime, equipment, or facilities. But very few spend the necessary time on strategy and creativity. Ideas are bigger than programs. Ideas are bigger than sermons. Ideas can change the world, so value their power.

4) Find Your Audience. Success isn't about being all things to all people. It's about being everything to some people. Jesus didn't win the entire world during his lifetime, and you won't either. So find the audience you can reach. Learn to match your gifts, talents, and passions to the particular audience that will respond to your message.

5) Understand the impact of an effective personal brand. A brand is your promise. A trusted brand influences culture, is innovative, has a distinct point of view, and delivers an experience. To discover your personal brand, ask 3 important questions: Who are you? In other words, what makes you, you. Second, what are your gifts and talents? What are you potentially the best at, and what motivates you? Third, what makes you unique? In other words, what separates you from the pack?

Once you can answer these questions, you begin the journey toward creating a unique perception in the audience's mind about who you are, what you have to say, and how you can change their lives. It's that distinctive perception that makes them want to listen to your message, and it's not that different from the reasons people buy certain products in the marketplace.

Perception is the beginning of your connection with an audience, and in a media driven world, controlling perception is critical.

Everything about how to get a message to an audience is changing in the 21st century. Yesterday it was about dumping the same message on the mass audience, and the audience had little choice. Today, it's about making a "connection" with the audience, the kind of connection that not only makes the audience want to hear what you have to say, but brings from it a response.

Stop giving your audience what you think it wants. Give it what it never dreamed it wanted.

The Media World is Changing

It has been a long and interesting road.

For more than a century, Christians have been taking the words and teachings of Christ to the world via what can be called a mass media. In many ways the history of the mass media - in America in particular - has also been the history of the Christian media. Just as the secular world began with the power and fascination of motion pictures, so did the church. At the turn of the century, Christians were some of the most prolific producers of movies in the country, and one of the first full length motion pictures was about the massive passion play in Oberramagau, Germany.

The next step was radio. According to the book, *Air of Salvation*, the National Religious Broadcasters 1994 landmark history of Christian media, by Mark Ward Sr., just months after the first secular radio broadcast (November 2, 1920) came the broadcast of a Sunday vespers service at Calvary Chapel in Pittsburgh, PA (January 2, 1921).

During the last thirty years, religious media has changed dramatically, and I've been privileged to be part of that change. When I began as a student in the 1970s, working on prime time TV specials for Oral Roberts, Christian television was surging in popularity. At that time, Oral Roberts was creating network quality prime time programs with popular special guests like Dionne Warwick, Robert Goulet, and Johnny Cash. Roberts had been on television since 1955 when he literally invented "paid-time broadcasting" with "The Abundant Life Program" on NBC, and now in the late 70's, he was easily the most popular regular, national broadcaster in Christian television.

He never asked for money, focused on family entertainment with an inspired message, and during those days of only three major networks, reached a staggeringly large audience. Peggy George, media buyer at the time for Oral Roberts Ministries, recalls that ratings varied according to the season and the special, but averaged 25 to 40 million viewers. Ms. George remembers, "This was a time before significant cable penetration and with very few religious stations, which we rarely used because of their low audience figures. I remember that our Sunday morning programs reached 4 million at the peak, running mostly at 9 or 9:30 a.m., and we were consistently the top-rated religious program against other ministers like Rex Humbard, Robert Schuller, Jimmy Swaggart, and Jim Bakker."

It was another era, indeed.

In those days, the Oral Roberts Ministry purchased the first three RCA cameras off the production line. They represented the cutting edge video technology of the time. The first camera was named the "Evelyn II" in honor of Roberts' wife. At the time, we pioneered the recording of all cameras and then synching them to edit, called

"ISO" recording. This revolutionized the way multi-camera television was directed and edited.

Since Oral couldn't be scripted and was totally spontaneous, recording the program on a single videotape machine was a real risk. You never knew what to expect with Oral, so we developed a system (revolutionary at the time) that allowed us to record (or ISO) every camera on the set. It was complicated and difficult to work out – especially with up to six cameras, but today it is standard on every multi-camera television program.

On a much smaller scale, local Christian broadcasting was beginning across the country, as people like Pat Robertson in Virginia, Claude Bowers in Florida, Blackie Gonzales in New Mexico, Russ Bixler in Pittsburgh, and Paul Crouch in California began buying TV stations in local markets and creating programming.

On all levels, it was a remarkable time. There was little controversy within religious media in those early days. Budgets with national programs were large enough to produce just about anything, and the impact was enormous.

But the world has changed. Cable television splintered the three major broadcast networks into multiple channels. As I write this, our cable company in Los Angeles offers 500 channels, and even the most remote places in America can access multiple channels through various cable or satellite providers.

In spite of that splintering of the industry, the growth of Christian media has been nothing short of a spiritual phenomenon. Today there are multiple networks devoted solely to Christian programming on the radio, television, and now the Internet. Nearly any hour of the day or night, one can tune in a religious program on some form of media anywhere in the United States, and most places in the world. Cross-country drivers can hear gospel music and teaching on their car radios. Teaching, preaching, even Christian entertainment programming can be found in nearly every market of the western world.

And a related revolution is also now in evidence. All across the Internet one can find Christian content, from news and commentary aimed at believers, to Christian-oriented blogs, chat rooms, and short films.

As a "preacher's kid," who grew up in the church, I witnessed these changes first-hand. As a media professional and television producer for more than a quarter century, both in the secular and Christian media, I have been involved as Christian media has refined its approach, and raised the level of quality, producing more effective and successful programming with each passing year. I was recently interviewed by an Australian television network about how increased production quality has impacted Christian broadcasting.

However, I also know that we are in a time of reappraisal, a period when we must take a new and critical look at the electronic, evangelistic tool that we have created.

It seems only a few years ago Christian preachers and teachers were encouraging creative young people to take a "new" approach and move into the media, where they could reach multitudes in numbers that the Apostles could only dream of. But, that time was nearly half a century ago. So, while we have to continue to encourage Christians to use the media to spread the Gospel, we must also make sure we haven't become complacent, and sloppy with the media tools we have. We must be certain that we haven't fallen into old habits that take the sting out of our revolutionary outreach.

Give Your Outreach a Tune-up

I can assure you that if you are a Christian media professional and haven't taken a hard, critical look at your church media outreach in the last year, you've got problems.

Technology changes, culture changes, trends change, people change, taste changes, and if you're not keeping up, then the effectiveness of your outreach is suffering.

Someone once said: "The message never changes, but the methods do." Yes, Jesus Christ is the same yesterday, today, and forever. But our camera and sound equipment, our staff, and our program ideas shouldn't be the same. So what are the steps to rethinking a media ministry to find the "new" again?

For a quick answer I would suggest the following:

1) Take a fresh look at advancing technology. When was the last time you attended the National Religious Broadcasters Convention or the National Association of Broadcasters Convention? These are places to see all the emerging technologies and talk to company officials, sales representatives and experienced producers. Stay ahead of the technology and how to use it.

2) Review your management skills. Take a look at your relationship with the people you manage. Sadly, one of the most prevalent problems in churches and ministries across the country is poor management. Remember, your people will do their best and most inspired work when you can clearly articulate your vision. Stop criticizing people and start patting them on the back – you'll be amazed at the difference it will make!

3) Develop relationships with other Christian media professionals. No one is an expert at everything. Don't reinvent the wheel. If you really want to grow and expand your outreach, learn from others who are already doing good work. Watch other Christian programs and find out who does what you need. Then don't be afraid to call and ask for advice.

4) Be different! Audiences are tired of worn-out set pieces, the same boring video effects, and trite phrases that litter typical Christian programs. In the advertising industry, we have a phrase: "Cutting through the clutter." Today, if you're going to find and keep an audience, you need to *cut through the clutter* and make your program different from all the other programs out there.

5) Make a new commitment to creativity. Start exercising your creative muscles. Look at new options, ideas, and program segments. Encourage your team to be more creative. You don't have to re-vamp every aspect of your broadcast outreach overnight, but at least start experimenting in small steps.

This checklist won't transform your media outreach overnight, but if you begin following each step, it won't be long before you see a significant change in the quality of your programming and the effectiveness of your media ministry.

Remember: The key is to review this checklist every six to 12 months, to stay in top creative, production, and management form.

But, beyond this important annual appraisal, my years of consulting for media ministries have taught me that there are additional questions and concerns that are common to most ministries. In the next few pages we will deal with these common concerns, beginning with "What is the future of Christian media?"

Chapter 1

The Future

—∿—

Convergence.

This is the answer to one of the most common questions I am asked, "What is the next big wave in the future of the Christian media?"

Convergence is no secret. Convergence is a popular subject right now and has been for some time. Recently, *The Hollywood Reporter* dedicated an entire page of its industry newspaper to the subject. If you've read the business section of your local newspaper, or recently looked at national news magazines, you're bound to have encountered the term "convergence".

Look at the global realignment of major companies trying to pave the way for its arrival. AOL's merger with Time Warner, Disney's acquisition of ABC, DreamWorks' failed attempt to create "Pop.com," CBS, Disney, and ABC's new online network offerings, Microsoft's relentless grab for more and more web-based companies. Google and Yahoo making entertainment based partnerships. Disney and Pixar. Even cell phone companies like Verizon building entertainment divisions. These are all indications that big business understands the coming wave and wants to be in position to take advantage of the assault.

Simply put, "convergence" means coming together from different directions, especially a uniting or merging. For our purposes it means merging different forms of media into a seamless medium. In its simplest form, it means everything coming through one box.

Depending on whom you talk to, sometime in the next three to five years, *information* resources such as computers, PDA's and cell phones, and *entertainment* resources like radio and television will merge into a single unit. In essence, we will be able to surf the web, do our computing, and watch the latest television program or movie, all on the same piece of equipment.

A myriad of media organizations are now trying to do two things:

1) Develop a creative entertainment format that people will want to view in the context of a computer, cell, or other mobile environment.

2) Develop the broadly accepted technology that will become the standard of the industry. The company that develops the universally accepted technology that allows convergence will reap billions.

What about the Christian media? Where are the realignments and partnerships designed to take advantage of this new technology? Is anyone in Christian media following the lead of secular big business?

Historically, Christian media has almost always been behind the curve. Few will dispute that Christian media has rarely been perceived as truly innovative or cutting edge.

In this area, however, there could be serious consequences if we fail to act quickly.

What exactly are the possibilities? With *convergence*, the options are endless. A 500-channel universe? That's nothing.

For instance: *the local video store will soon be a thing of the past, because we can now download any movie in existence as easy as we download our e-mail.* Proof? Blockbuster Home Video has recently announced that video rentals are on their way out, and Blockbuster stores will be offering a host of other options, including satellite dishes, and equipment for downloading movies off the Internet. Record labels are experimenting with dumping CD packaging in favor of customers coming to a record store and downloading a new CD directly into a personal music player.

We can finally make television programs truly interactive. Proof? From the earliest episodes of the program, you could access the "American Idol" website and play (or vote) along with the television program. And network executives are working on an interactive system that will allow that to happen right on the television screen.

We can videoconference anywhere on the planet. Proof? In most places, it's old news. But as wireless communications companies grow more compatible worldwide, we'll be able to videoconference from the Sahara Desert as easily as Wall Street. When my wife Kathleen and I sent our daughter across the country to college, I gave her a webcam so we could keep in touch visually through her instant messaging software.

Now we can find out immediate and accurate information about who's watching particular programs and why. Proof? Look at the growing list of companies specializing in accurate audience reporting for web-based applications and programs.

Literally millions of music, movie, television program, book, website, and other entertainment choices will soon be at our fingertips. Proof? Check out websites such as: ifilm.com, youtube.com, current.tv, atomfilms.com and more. (New sites are popping up overnight).

What Does this Mean for Christians?

But, now back to the critical question: **What does this mean to Christians?** How can we, as Christians, be ready to use this new medium, or combination of old media, for presenting a message of hope to a world desperately in need? To incorporate these new media combinations into your ministry, you must:

1) Understand that convergence is actually here. Before you as a Christian media professional can understand convergence, you must deal with the word *change.* You must understand that if Christians don't understand and utilize this technology, they will become the dinosaurs of the digital age. Perhaps the best way to start is to partner with creative Christian producers and designers who understand the potential of the web and be willing to fund some experimental projects with them. Could we fail? Of course! But if we don't get in the game, we'll *never* have a chance to win.

2) Invest in the Digital Age. Remember: Good stewardship isn't just saving money; it's investing money in the right places. Begin to invest in equipment and people that can help you reach into the digital future.

3) Progress from the age of TV preachers to the age of media producers. Preachers were the pioneers of Christian media. However, the media world of today is vastly different from the '40s and '50s. And yet, most Christian radio and television stations are still broadcasting mostly sermon-based programming.

Of course there will always be a place on Christian media for powerful and anointed preaching. But if we're going to be successful in the *age of convergence*, we have to think more creatively about our programming.

That's why the simple techniques of storytelling are as important as ever. Certain new technologies – for example, the ability to move between the Internet and television, add a hyperlink to a movie, or integrate moving video into websites – will allow us to tell our stories as never before. Essentially, storytelling hasn't changed from the time Hebrew storytellers sat around campfires in the desert passing on the stories that became the Old Testament. But now, we have new tools to make our storytelling more compelling and effective.

The issues of "convergence" can be both frightening and exhilarating. But if you stay near the heart of God in your decision-making, and seek the help and counsel of godly men and women along with experienced media professionals, your chances of success will be greatly increased.

We are standing at the door of a historic new period. As Christians, this can be our chance to break through with a message of hope to this culture. Let's take that next step with authority and boldness, knowing that we worship a God who is the ultimate Creator. Following His lead is our key to success.

But back to the critical question: "What does this mean to Christians?

Numerous innovative believers are already developing new concepts and ideas for mobile communications, such as fully functioning websites for cell phones, including ministry programming. Our company, Cooke Pictures, has been instrumental in developing programming for the web, including teaching resources, entertainment, and information-based programs. One ministry is creating a web-based resource for a wide range of personal and family challenges, including help with addictions, abuse, and other issues.

One of the most important ideas I've tried to communicate to pastors and ministry leaders is that a website should be much more than simply a bio of the pastor, doctrinal principles, and a map to the church. In the new web 2.0 – the current technological evolution of the Internet - a contemporary site can host audio and video clips, interactive features, online communities, online blogs and more – all designed to develop a relationship with the user and build a connection with the congregation or ministry partners. In fact, recent studies reveal that for teens today, "digital space" is just as important for them as "meat space" (not my terms – but you get the point).

Keys to Convergence

To that end, I've developed seven "Keys" that I believe we as Christian media professionals need to make an impact in the age of convergence. These are important principles that will help create a more effective message within the context of this new medium, and help you cut through the clutter and advertising hype that surrounds the world of convergence:

Key #1 – Understand the power of telling a story. As usual, most churches and ministries want to begin with equipment and technology, but I always prefer to begin with *the story*. Ultimately, no matter what communications medium we choose, that's all we're doing – *telling a story*. A simple story about how God *chose to become one of us to share His eternal plan with people who didn't deserve it.*

That's it.

As we enter the digital age of convergence, let's spend more time learning how to tell a story more effectively. It doesn't matter so much the program format – *preaching, music, documentary, variety, drama, whatever* – every program is telling some type of story, and until that story is told most effectively, the audience is never going to be interested.

This Sunday, thousands of pastors will step into the pulpit and not tell a single story. Yet when you study the life of Jesus, that's just about all he did. He rarely lectured or preached – he mostly told stories. These stories touched people, and changed lives.

The great Swedish filmmaker Ingmar Bergman said: *"Facts go straight to the head, and stories go straight to the heart."*

There's no question that our storytelling abilities can be greatly challenged and expanded with the advent of convergence. The ability to crisscross between the Internet and a television program, add a hyperlink to a movie, integrate moving video into websites, or create active, online communities, allow us to tell our stories as never before. But don't allow links, transitions, and other gimmicks to distract you from the need to tell a story.

Remember, the medium doesn't matter as much as the message.

In the age of convergence, let's make a new commitment to storytelling, and understand that unless we can tell a powerful story, our chance of reaching an audience is terribly diminished.

Key #2 – Be In Touch With the Current Culture. I find that a remarkable number of pastors, evangelists, and church leaders are out of touch with today's culture. Don't believe me? Go on the web and use a search engine to find *Christian youth sites.* You won't believe the terrible websites you'll find. Some have excellent resources for young people, but their graphic presentation is so out of style, no young person would even consider looking at the site.

Christian producers often don't keep up with current programming and graphic styles, and I'm amazed at the number of Christian media professionals who never watch television. If we're going to make an impact in this culture, we have to understand what makes it tick. Just as Paul in Acts 17 used his knowledge of Greek literature and culture to establish a "common ground" with the philosophers on Mars Hill, we need to understand the music, literature, films, and television that this culture creates. Otherwise, they will continue to believe that our message is irrelevant and unimportant. Remember, when it comes to the age of convergence, it's not worth doing if it's not done in a style and language this culture understands.

Key #3 – Make sure your financing is in place. Most Christian producers are plagued with a lack of funds for media production and equipment. Television, for instance, is probably the most expensive outreach your church or ministry will ever encounter, and poor decisions regarding financing can literally destroy entire ministry organizations. I always recommend that you have six months to a year of funding in the bank before beginning a media outreach. On most cable systems, there are a minimum of 70-plus channels, which means there is lots of competition. So it takes between six months to a year of broadcasting before your program begins to establish itself with its audience. In the world of convergence, the number of "channels" is potentially endless, and the competition is even greater. That means it could be years before you receive any significant response or financial support from your audience – *they simply need time to find the program.*

Therefore, it's critical that you are able to fund your program at least during that first year, or your media ministry will never have the chance to make an impact.

Key #4 – Be open to change. The unexpected is often the most exciting and effective answer! In Hollywood, millions of dollars are spent every year on "pilot" programs – many of which never see the light of day. For all practical purposes, pilots are the research and development departments of studios and networks. They understand that audiences are always changing, so they aren't afraid to experiment and update programs and ideas. But most Christian programs are doing the same thing they did 10 to 15 years ago, and most Christian websites rarely get updated. (Speaking of websites, remember that if a person returns to your site once and the content hasn't changed, they probably won't come back again.) In the age of convergence, the most successful media ministries will be ministries that aren't afraid to change, update, and present a fresh, new approach to an ever-changing audience.

Key #5 – Don't forget creativity. An advertising executive once said: *"Creativity is like shaving – if you don't do it every day, you're a bum!"* Exercise those creative muscles and do it on a regular basis. Don't take the easy way out, either in sermon preparation or program production. I don't buy the theory that only a few of us are born "creative". I believe anyone can be more creative. It just takes practice, and a willingness to forgo the "easy" way. Be open to new and better ideas.

A recent research study revealed that creative people aren't necessarily special; they simply work harder at being innovative. Truth is, creativity is the currency of this culture. In Hollywood, the creative jobs are the highest paid, because the secular entertainment and media industries understand its value. When an audience has the option to view almost unlimited channels of information and entertainment in the age of convergence, creativity will be a key element that brings that audience to you.

Key #6 – Don't limit your vision to preaching. As I've said, preaching is a wonderful thing, and there will always be room in Christian media for good, solid preaching. But one of my greatest disappointments is that many Christian Internet sites are nothing more than an archive of old video and audio clips of sermons. We already know that Christian television has largely been a depository for videotaped sermons, and a church service doesn't necessarily make the best television. Remember, a light bulb isn't just a candle you plug into the wall. A car isn't a horse with wheels, and a television isn't a radio with pictures. Shooting a church service with three or four cameras doesn't necessarily make it a compelling television program.

When you're in a church service or evangelistic event, you can feel the electricity of the crowd, you can see the emotion and intensity of the speaker, and you can experience the live event with the enthusiasm and excitement of hundreds or thousands of other people. However, when you watch that same event on television, you're often sitting alone in a room, watching on a "glass box" 10 or 15 feet away. You're probably also having a meal, talking with a friend, getting dressed, or reading. *Believe me, it's not the same experience.* In fact, it's such a problem that advertisers call it "cutting through the clutter." They are referring to the ability to create programming that cuts through all the distractions and makes an impact on its audience.

Don't forget other program types that are remarkably absent from most Christian media, such as documentaries, movies, children's programs, news, animation and music. Remember, the secular networks spend millions of dollars to find out what audiences will watch, and if you check the latest prime time schedule it's filled with movies, episodic dramas, reality programs and situation comedies – nowhere on the schedule can you find someone standing behind a pulpit just talking. Certainly there are executives in Hollywood who are biased against people of faith, as is often claimed. However, I really don't believe that most secular networks hate Christians. These networks just want to *make money* (and would probably sell their grandmother to do it).

Remember the secular networks profit from selling advertising time, so if they felt preaching shows would draw a significant audience, I'm convinced they would have preaching shows in prime time. But they know the power of story-based programs, and thus fill the television schedule with that format.

Key #7 – Don't underestimate the importance of quality. Many Christian churches and ministries don't understand the need to produce high quality media outreaches. Today's audiences are more technologically sophisticated than ever. They refuse to watch programs that aren't up to current standards. Remember my earlier comment about most cable systems having at least 70 channels? The virtually unlimited-channel universe is not far around the corner. In this convergence environment, it's too easy to change the channel or website if the picture, graphic style, or audio quality isn't satisfying.

Commit to Quality

I'll say it many times in this book: *Stewardship* isn't just saving money; it's also *using money more effectively*. Sometimes that means spending more money to purchase a better product that will help reach your goals sooner and more effectively.

Many churches and ministries purchase cheap equipment in order to save money, but soon discover they should have waited until they could afford better quality. Don't let your desire to get on radio, television or the Internet push you into getting low quality or inferior equipment. After all, you can't reach the lost if they won't watch long enough to hear your message.

Quality not only involves equipment, it involves people as well. I will deal with this in more detail in Chapter 3, but I believe it is also important to this discussion. I know one pastor in the South who spent two million dollars to upgrade his television equipment to high definition standards, but used volunteers run the operation. Traditionally, pastors and ministry leaders value equipment more than people. If you give the finest computer in the world to the average person in your congregation, he or she still wouldn't be able to write a best-selling novel. You need to bring in the best media professionals you can afford to help you with your television ministry. Where do you find them? Here are a few places:

a) At professional conferences like *The Technologies for Worship Conference* sponsored by *Technologies for Worship* magazine, usually held in association with the National Association of Broadcasters Conference in Las Vegas.

b) Through professional organizations like the *National Religious Broadcasters* in Manassas, Virginia.

c) By asking the leadership at a church or ministry with a media outreach you admire.

d) By inquiring at Christian colleges. They often have Communication Departments with majors in radio, television, and multimedia, and know qualified alumni in your area.

Just because your brother-in-law loves your ministry and is a loyal family member doesn't mean he's the best person to help you build an effective and successful media outreach. Find godly people who have a genuine calling to reach the world through media. Not only can they help you save money and time, they can also make a dramatic difference in the success of your media ministry.

Post the "7 Keys" listed above in your office to remind you of your commitment to principles that will help launch your media ministry into the age of convergence and keep you focused on your goal.

Surviving and succeeding in a converged media world.

Over the course of my career in the media, I've had the opportunity to visit hundreds of churches, ministries, and Christian organizations and helped them face a multitude of media challenges. Over those nearly three decades, I've discovered five major areas of leadership that have to be confronted over and over again. I believe we may never make a real impact on this culture unless we can confront these critical challenges and overcome them.

All of us have a place in the greater plan of God to reach the lost. The key to making this happen is to understand the playing field. What are the challenges we face? Who are the players? What resources are available to us? What mistakes have others made? What position can we best fill?

Once we discover the answers to these questions, we can really begin to move forward.

My father was an all-state football player in high school, but in his younger years it took awhile for him to find the right position on the team. As a result, he spent time on the bench. One year, dad's team was in the playoffs, and as usual he was sitting while everyone else was playing. In a crucial play, the quarterback was hit hard and suddenly went down. A hush fell over the home team stands as the quarterback was helped off the field surrounded by players and coaches.

That's when the head coach looked down the long, lonely bench and yelled at my father: "Cooke! Get over here!"

He excitedly got up and ran over to the head coach. Strangely though, the coach took him around to the side of the stands. The coach told Dad: "Listen, the starting quarterback got hit on that last play and split his pants. You're his size, so he needs your pants to finish the game."

Dad reluctantly exchanged pants with the quarterback and walked back to the bench with a towel around his waist. The quarterback went back into the game.

Different people are called to different levels of leadership, but the key principles are always the same. My dad started his football career humbly giving up his pants, but went on to be the best in the state at his position. So, no matter where we start, we need to do it humbly, but with a sense of purpose.

That's why understanding these *five guiding principles of leadership* is so critical.

1) Leaders must passionately embrace higher quality leadership. I've had the opportunity to work with literally hundreds of organizations over the years, both Christian and secular, and I've decided that there are more management dysfunctions in Christian organizations than anywhere else on the planet. Sure companies like Enron have achieved mythic status because of massive and tragic mismanagement, but the fact is that most American businesses are managed far better than most churches, ministries and ministry organizations.

For years we've *talked* about leadership within Christian media circles, but in reality we haven't done much about it. I work as a consultant with many organizations, so I get to hear a variety of perspectives – from the guy in shipping all the way up to the head of the ministry. Do I get visionary, loyal, fired-up, cutting edge responses? Rarely. I usually get gripes, frustrations, anger and the sense that people are being used without any consideration for their gifts, teamwork and real abilities.

So what can we do? First, we need to understand real leadership. Are we reading books by those whom God has given deep insights into leadership issues? Do we know the principles of true leadership and how to create an atmosphere where people will gladly face any obstacle to accomplish the vision?

We must hire people based on gifts and talents – not based on the strength of their testimonies, hard luck stories, loyalty, or their relatives. Of course we care about people, and of course we want to help. But we *must* remember the words of Jack Welch, legendary CEO of General Electric: "If you leave someone in a position they can't handle – even out of kindness – you not only hurt the organization, you hurt the person involved. You're giving the worker a false sense of accomplishment, and keeping them from discovering the real place where their gifts and talents can be used."

Read that quote again.

I know of one ministry with a key employee who was so incompetent, she was costing the ministry nearly $100,000 a year. Through missed deadlines, poor quality work, mistakes, and more, she was draining the organization, and because other employees knew it, morale was plummeting.

And yet, for years the ministry failed to act out of a misplaced sense of loyalty.

I love loyal employees, but like Jack Welch says, if they're failing, they not only hurt the organization, they hurt themselves as well. Very often, the best thing you can do for a failing employee is to help them move on to a place where they can find a better fit.

Finally, we need to understand what business we're in. When it comes to the media, we're not so much in the "ministry" business; we're in the "influence" business. Our job is to influence people with a new way of thinking to change their circumstances and transform their destinies. But, how much do we know about influence? How much do we know about the principles of communication that lead to someone changing their perspective, and changing their viewpoint?

I don't think you'll get a homosexual man to change his lifestyle by calling him ugly names on national TV. But, that's exactly what some organizations do. I don't think you'll get people to change their attitudes about abortion by constantly hammering on the people who get abortions. But, that's exactly what some organizations do.

I've said before that it's time we moved from the era of radio and TV *preachers* to the era of media *producers*. For years, the people in front of the microphone and in front of the camera have controlled Christian media. Frankly, they've usually done a great job and are the undisputed pioneers of this industry. While many of us were sitting on our duff, it was preachers who were out presenting the gospel on radio, television, even in movies and now the Internet.

But, I believe that era has come to a close. Because of changes in the media landscape, the complexity and expense of projects, the need to expand our creativity and a better understanding of the techniques for reaching audiences, control of what we do needs to come from behind the microphone and camera.

I'm the first to agree that good preaching is fantastic. But it's only *one* way to reach the mass audience. We now understand the power of documentaries, music programming, comedy, drama, reality and experimental projects.

Believe me, I've learned from experience working with hundreds of pastors and evangelists that when you're a hammer, you see everything as a nail. To a preacher every problem can be solved by a good sermon. Preachers are wired for that. It's their gift, and I love them for it.

But, we who sit behind the camera and microphone can see a much bigger picture. We understand that what Christian media is doing right now is only a small part of how we can reach this culture in this new millennium.

To reach this culture we have to develop INFLUENCE. That's why leaders must passionately embrace higher quality leadership.

2) Leaders must passionately embrace creative thinking. We're losing the culture war because our competitors are telling better stories than we are. Let's face it – we work in the industry, yet how many of us race home from work so we can enjoy our favorite Christian TV or radio program? I've always thought it odd that the TV viewing habits of Christians are virtually identical to non-believers. Even Christians don't watch us. We're being out-thought by the secular world and it shows in the creative aspects of the programs we produce.

I'm sick to death of people pitching me programs with the line: "What we need is a Christian version of 'Oprah." Or, "Have you seen Jay Leno? Why can't we do a Christian version of that?"

I'll tell you why I hate it, because we ought to be doing so much better! We worship the ultimate Creator of the universe, and yet our creativity stinks!

My dream is to walk down the corridors at a major Hollywood studio and overhear a conversation from the executives that goes something like this: "You know, what we need is a *secular* version of this really great program I saw on a *Christian* network last night."

Recently, I watched some old tapes from the '50s of Christian broadcasters like Fulton Sheen and Oral Roberts. You know what? It is more than 50 years later and our programs pretty much follow the same old format, with the same preaching style. We're in color now, but that's pretty much the only difference. I was amazed that in 50 years our creative values have not progressed beyond that.

Some will say: *"My program may not be the most creative, but it's the content that counts"*.

Actually, no it's not.

Research and my own professional experience have shown me that television audiences today only take between three and five (yes, that's 3 and 5!) seconds to decide whether or not to watch your program. If you've sat on the sofa with a remote in your hands, you know I'm telling the truth (especially you men). At my home in Los Angeles, I already have nearly 500 channels and my wife will confirm that I probably only give each one about two seconds max. So, once again, it doesn't matter how heartfelt your message if the audience doesn't watch long enough to hear it you've failed.

That's why leaders must passionately embrace creative thinking – to quickly capture the attention of the audience.

3) Leaders must passionately understand the culture. When I was growing up in the '50s and '60s in the South, the pulpit determined the behavior of the country. My dad was a pastor and was the most respected guy in our community. Even people who would never consider coming to church still respected my dad and his principles because the church had real authority. But today, movies and prime-time television determine the moral climate of this country. Teenagers learn most of their behavior not from school, or from friends, or even from parents. Instead they buy into the behavior they're shown on television and in the movies. Therefore, if we don't have a voice in those arenas, we won't make much of an impact.

Today, popular culture is the heartbeat of this country. (Why do you think they call it "popular?") Paul understood the power of culture when he approached the philosophers in Athens in Acts 17. Sure, he could have said: *"I'm going to preach the gospel, and I'm going to preach it without compromise no matter what."* But he didn't do that. He respected their culture, their values and their ideas. Once he won their respect he was able to reach them in a far deeper way.

MTV has captured the hearts and minds of our young people. You don't have to like its programming, but you must know how it works? If you have a heart to reach young people, you need to know how MTV, Nickelodeon and other successful companies have so much influence. Do you know why Nike, Budweiser and other companies produce successful advertising?

Again, leaders must passionately understand the culture.

4) Leaders must passionately embrace financial opportunities. Now, before you think I'm going to start preaching about giving, let me explain what I believe true prosperity/affluence/wealth really is. I believe real prosperity is whatever divine provision is necessary for us to accomplish what God has called us to do. The media world is a very expensive business. Trying to reach people with the gospel on a regional, national or international scale takes a lot of money.

The truth is, money is a critical key to our future. For instance, I really believe we can talk about production values, creativity and technical issues all day long, but the person who changes Christian television will be the person who changes the way it's funded. As long as we're following the historic paid-time model and asking for money on the air, we're never going to get the level of funding needed to produce high quality specials, documentaries, music programming, or movies. If that model works for you, great, but it doesn't really work for most Christian producers and programmers.

That's why I'm concerned that we're not putting enough effort into financial issues in Christian media. In Hollywood, you see first-hand how much effort the studios and networks put into financial issues, because funding drives the business.

Isn't it interesting that the most sketchy and controversial Bible teaching you'll find on Christian television often comes during telethon week? The pressure to get the phones to ring creates some pretty bizarre programming.

And you'd be amazed at the number of ministries that teach prosperity, but are still the biggest tightwads. They pay their people minimum wage, and rarely give them a raise, financial incentives, or other monetary considerations. Don't bleed your people dry. Value what they bring to the table. (If they don't bring anything to the table, maybe you've hired the wrong person.) Stop paying a fortune for equipment while expecting people to work for nothing.

Also, find a successful Christian businessperson in your area and start spending time with them. Successful businesspeople think differently. They value different things, and we can learn so much from their perspectives.

I know of a Christian station manager who has begun partnerships with successful businesspeople in his community. He spends time with them mining their experience, advice and expertise. As a result they have helped him get loans, develop credit lines with banks, get equipment at discount prices, find free donations from vendors, hire qualified staff, and learn visionary thinking. It has totally changed everything about the way the station operates. They've gone from a poverty mentality to a success mentality almost overnight.

That's why leaders must passionately embrace financial opportunities to accomplish what God has called them to do.

5) Finally, leaders must passionately embrace planting seeds. No, I'm not going to take up an offering. Today, most ministry organizations are obsessed with "the harvest." They're obsessed with numbers, salvations and mailing lists. On the surface, all that sounds great. But according to the Bible and the laws of nature, a harvest can't happen without planting seeds. When the Bible talks about harvests, it either states or implies that the harvest came because someone had previously planted seeds, watered, and tended the crop.

My Ph.D. dissertation was a study of cinema and theology. During the dissertation process I studied *The Engel Scale*, a chart created by Dr. James Engel when he was with the Billy Graham School of Evangelism. Dr. Engel identifies eight clear steps a person goes through in the process of accepting Christ. He shows that finding salvation is really a *process*, not a one-decision event. One major crusade ministry told me of an informal survey they conducted of people who had accepted Christ at their crusades over a one-year period. Person after person, the survey revealed that each one had been confronted with the gospel message an average of 17 times before they finally made "the decision."

Others planted an average of 17 seeds before there was a harvest.

Tim Downs has written a remarkable book: "*Finding Common Ground: How to Communicate with Those Outside the Christian Community... While We Still Can.*" He gives a wonderful example of two young Christian men who go seeking financial support from the Missions Committee at their local church. One wants to go into "the mission field," while the other wants to attend the "UCLA Film School." Guess which one gets the money? The missionary, of course – even though the Film School student has the potential of reaching far more people with the gospel through the media.

We have to change the thinking of the church when it comes to evangelism. That's why leaders must passionately embrace planting seeds.

To recap, leaders must passionately embrace:
- *Higher Quality Leadership*
- *Creative Thinking*
- *Understanding the Culture*
- *Financial Opportunities*
- *Planting Seeds*

What will that do? It will show us how to lead the industry to more creative and effective programming, penetrate the culture with the gospel, find the funding to accomplish our goals and learn the process that leads to a more effective harvest.

And for me, that's what it's all about.

When my dad tells the story of giving his football pants to the quarterback so the team could continue the game, he never fails to mention that on the very next play the quarterback ran 40 yards for the winning touchdown.

And with a proud gleam in his eye, my dad adds: "And he did it in my pants!"

When it comes to the media, we're not all major players. I wouldn't be considered a quarterback or even a blocker. Maybe all some of us can do is donate our pants. But whatever leadership role God calls us to, if we master these five areas, we dramatically enhance our ability to impact this generation.

Chapter 2

The Power of Perception

—∿—

Remember, it's not just who you are, or what you are trying to say. It's how you and your message are perceived that matters.

Today, when researchers study the process of communication, they realize the message being sent is not always the message being received. In fact, few communicated messages actually arrive with the same intentions, information, and impact. Jesus understood that perception is a powerful thing, with enormous consequences and therefore was very sensitive to the audience he was addressing.

I am frequently asked by media ministers, "How can I combat a negative perception within the audience I am trying to reach? One of the first signs that you need to change the approach you are taking with your media ministry is when you realize your ministry has a negative perception within your potential audience.

Criticism can be the best gauge of your audience's perception. Check your mail, e-mails, and local news stories from time to time. Certainly some will be critical no matter what you do, but if you read your critical mail with a desire to improve, you'll find a remarkable number of areas where people can misunderstand your message, or walk away with the wrong impression of you, your church, or your ministry.

Some pastors have a "post-Sunday debriefing" with their leadership team, focusing on questions like: "How did people respond to the service?" "Was there criticism from within the congregation?" "How can we more effectively help people understand the message we are trying to get across?" "Were the media tools we used effective?"

Too many pastors and ministry leaders refuse to listen to criticism, and the sad fact is, most major media ministries that have crashed over the years became susceptible when their leaders insulated themselves from hearing and responding to legitimate criticism. Certainly you want to keep criticism in perspective, but I'm always a bit suspicious of pastors and ministry leaders who never listen to anything negative.

So the question becomes, how can we control the perceptions of others? To what extent can we influence the way others perceive us, and how can we honestly express our faith and accomplish our calling, and still keep control of the way the world sees us?

First, we must understand that perception can be a positive tool. The fact is, many people have misused the power of perception, and our culture suffers the consequences. But in spite of the abuse, the power of perception can be utilized for good, if we learn how to activate it in our lives.

Start by thinking in reverse. It's not the message you send that counts; it's the message that's received. Whether you're communicating on the job, preaching a sermon, talking with your family, or sharing your faith in some other way, realize that every listener is evaluating your message through his or her own life experiences, which determine to a great extent the impact it will have on them.

For instance, when you preach on adultery or divorce, someone who's suffered the pain of betrayal will react very differently from someone who's been happily married for twenty years, or someone who's never been married at all.

Don't begin this process with your message. Begin with knowing the person on the other end of your communication. That's why research is so important. I encourage our clients to learn everything they can about the audience. Not because we want to compromise or cater to the lowest common denominator, but because we want that audience to respond to and benefit from the message. You communicate far more effectively with your own family than you do with strangers because you know their likes and dislikes, what gets them excited, what motivates them, and more. That's why advertisers spend millions of dollars on research before they shoot television commercials. They want to make sure that their spot has the greatest impact.

Another important key is to remember the importance of "packaging." When I was a kid, there were only three channels on the television, but on our cable system today in Los Angeles, my children choose from 500 channels. I use this example so frequently, because it illustrates such an important issue. It's why, how a program looks and sounds, the special effects used, the stars – the "packaging," – is just as important as the content. Therefore, no matter how brilliant or anointed the program, if it's not packaged in a compelling way, the viewer won't watch long enough to hear the message.

Start by thinking about your personal packaging. Do you dress appropriately? Do you express yourself well? Do you communicate confidence when you meet people? How's your grammar? Are you growing in your skills?

What does this mean to your ministry?

It's really not the principles of the Christian faith that garner most of the world's criticism. Rather, it's how the church practices its faith, how it causes (or allows) itself to be perceived. The history of the faith is littered with men and women who may have been sincere and genuine, but because they cared little for how they were perceived, they ended up doing far more damage than good. To avoid perpetuating this:

1) Understand that how you are perceived is critical. It doesn't matter if you're a brilliant pastor or executive, if people believe you're a loser or a jerk. Take the time and effort to manage their perceptions, so you and your gifts can be positioned in the best possible light. It's not about ego or manipulation; it's about creating an environment where you're appreciated, not tolerated. Remember: If you don't control your perception, you'll always be at the mercy of others who will.

2) Remember, God called us to be a light within our culture, because light draws people – it doesn't repel them. Everyday at the office, in school, in our homes, and with our neighbors, we have the opportunity to impact people's perception of God and His ability to impact their lives. And unless they perceive "the faith's" ability to make a difference, they'll never take a critical step toward that faith.

But, how do we discern the difference between our attempts to influence others for good, and our own ego?

That becomes an issue of integrity. It requires daily pursuing the God of Truth and seeking to express His purpose in every association, project, or relationship. Only God can change hearts, but he allows us the gift of being active in His plan. King David said: "Some trust in chariots, and some in horses: but we will remember the name of the LORD our God."

Understand the power of perception, but never forget that God is ultimately in control. A negative perception can be overcome, but it will take real effort.

Finding a new approach

Ultimately, the success of our message is determined when the listener or viewer makes a decision. That's why if it becomes clear that your current approach to media ministry is not being well received in the marketplace, it is time to make some changes. It is impossible for me to offer an easy answer to what changes you should make, and make no mistake, *there is no silver bullet*. Media ministry is a complex task and no one has all the answers. On the secular side, Hollywood spends hundreds of millions of dollars each season on new television programs and movies. Most fail.

Any major change in approach will depend on a host of variables. For instance, the type of audience you are trying to reach, the resources you have, the type and training level of your personnel, the budget you are working within, your program structure, your product or resource offers, all these and a variety of other things figure in to a choice of a new approach.

I can offer a few general options, however.

If you are now using a traditional preaching format, you might experiment with some of the well-established commercial broadcast structures, which have only recently gotten wide use in Christian circles. Try something like traditional advertising, direct response or reality programming.

A basic advertising lesson

A male friend recently sent me the following in an email. Using a little humor, it imparts some important information about different types of advertising.

You see a gorgeous girl at a party. You go up to her and say: "I'm the man of your dreams." <u>That's Direct Marketing</u>.

You're at a party with a bunch of friends and see a gorgeous girl. One of your friends goes up to her and, pointing at you, says: "He's the man of your dreams." <u>That's advertising</u>.

You see a gorgeous girl at a party. You go up to her and get her telephone number. The next day you call and say: "Hi, I'm the man of your dreams." <u>That's Telemarketing</u>.

You're at a party and see a gorgeous girl. You get up and straighten your tie, then walk up to her and offer to get her a drink. You open the door for her, pick up her bag after she drops it, offer her a ride, and then say: "By the way, I'm the man of your dreams." <u>That's Public Relations</u>.

You're at a party and see a gorgeous girl. She walks up to you and says: "I hear you're the man of my dreams." <u>That's Brand Recognition</u>."

End of lesson.

Madison Avenue advertising agencies spend billions each year on producing and broadcasting advertising spots. In our society, some commercials have even been elevated to the status of cultural icons. Why? Five important reasons:

1) The power of focus in advertising. Commercials focus an audience's attention for 30 to 60 seconds. With arresting visuals, powerful music and creative style, they make a strong impression by hitting hard and making an impact. That's why advertisers are willing to pay $2 million plus for a 30-second spot on the Super Bowl. Those 30 seconds of focus can dramatically change consumer behavior.

2) The flexibility of the advertising message. You can place ads in a great variety of time slots. Half-hour programs are often difficult to schedule, but spots can be dropped anywhere. Experts frequently experiment for maximum effect with spots, and try to reach different audiences at different time periods.

3) The relative economy of advertising. Ad spots are often much less expensive than producing and broadcasting full-length programs. So before you try a 30-minute infomercial-style program, you might experiment with a 30- or 60-second spot.

4) The high production value. Their shorter length allows for concentrated creativity and quality. In the ad world, every second counts, so directors try to make each shot more powerful than he or she could in a full-length program.

5) The cultural impact of advertising. Commercials are a part of the fabric of our culture. Spots are celebrated, honored, and have become cultural icons. In fact, the Museum of Modern Art in New York City has a permanent collection of each year's best commercials. This is a modern marketplace of ideas where the people discuss, debate, and mix it up. Highly creative spots are often the number one water cooler topic in offices across America.

Few churches and ministries really produce spots well. If your ads fall into that category, here's seven "commandments" for producing an effective commercial:

1) Make sure your spot is believable and compelling. It should sell, but it should sell with truth and honesty. You'll hear me talk about "authenticity" a lot in this book.

2) Remember, motivation is king. Entertainment is good, but make sure the spot is more motivational than entertaining. Entertainment is important and often causes people to recall the spot, but it should be a secondary goal.

3) Keep in mind the question: "What does the product or message actually do?" Describe your competitive advantage. Don't leave your audience confused about what you are offering.

4) Create strong visuals. On TV, visuals are far more important than sound; in fact, researchers find that up to 85 percent of a message's impact comes from the visuals (rather than from any aural stimuli).

5) Make the spot excellent. Create high production value. An advertising guru once said, "Nobody overtly pays attention to production values – unless they stink." Then they remember.

6) Create desire within your audience. At the end, no one should care about the TV spot. But they should want your "product" – your message.

7) Focus on advancing the sale, not being "cute." Think "product" and benefit.

Effective commercials create awareness, a higher profile, and a powerful impact. Explore the possibilities spots can give your church, ministry, or organization.

As a Christian, I once looked at the art of influencing perception as a negative, deceitful proposition. Indeed it can be, but like many things, I have learned it has a flip side. I began to study how Jesus went to great lengths to impact the public perception of his ministry and his purpose on earth.

He actually told people who had been healed not to tell anyone.

He carefully chose the men who would be His closest associates.

During the height of his popularity, he withdrew to remote places to be alone.

He chose the method of his triumphal entry into Jerusalem.

When He could have escaped in the garden, he told Peter to stop fighting and quietly allowed Himself to be arrested.

During the events that led to his execution, He even controlled the interrogation of Pilate by only responding to certain questions.

Jesus had a purpose and plan for his life, and he refused to let others determine his destiny or how He would be perceived.

But why did He care what people thought? Wouldn't Jesus Christ be concerned only with the truth? He dealt with truth, but he was careful to orchestrate how that truth was perceived.

That is similar to how we as Christians can use advertising to direct an audience to the faith.

In Christian media, we generally use four advertising types:

1) Image Advertising. This is an approach that doesn't directly sell a product or service, but places an "image" in the mind of the viewer. Some denominations use this method to create advertising that positions their churches in a positive way in the community.

2) Evangelism. This type of spot attempts to "sell" – but it doesn't sell a product. Its purpose is to make people stop and think, and hopefully, plant a seed, or make a decision for Christ. There have been a wide variety of these spots – some good, and others awkward and unbelievable – and it's probably been used most effectively by the Mormon Church. They have invested millions in their ongoing campaigns on television, and achieved excellent results in expanding their church's membership.

3) Public Service. These spots are usually produced and broadcast for free, and focus attention on some public need or cause – against smoking, increasing awareness and contributions to the fights against cancer, heart disease, homelessness, AIDS, etc. Typically sponsored by the government or public charities, advertising agencies usually do this work on a "pro bono" (free) basis. Innovative public service spots often win awards because the subject matter can encourage very creative approaches.

One of the most powerful public service spots was directed by controversial British director Tony Kaye (American History X) and featured a heroin user simply talking to the camera about how heroin wasn't really a problem, and he could quit at any time. But Kaye visually contrasted what the person was saying with shots of a filthy apartment, a soiled mattress, needle marks and sores on the addict's arm, his emaciated condition, and the fact that he did the entire interview standing in dirty, saggy, underwear. The visual approach said far more than his feeble dialogue, and the spot won numerous awards as a powerful indictment against drug abuse.

4) Direct Response Advertising. This is the most used style in Christian media, because it asks for an immediate response from the audience. It's used to sell books, teaching tapes, ministry tours, conferences, and many other things, and has proven very successful when executed correctly. The key to excellent DR is to realize that the era of cheesy, corny, "infomercial" style spots is over. Yes, there are a few remnants of bad stuff left out there, but in most cases, direct response can and should be high quality and stylish. The producer simply has to make the need evident, and provide the product that solves the problem. Most important, it needs to be done <u>right now</u>. Effective DR spots create an immediate need to have the problem solved – whether it is acne, a fat stomach, financial debt, or a better understanding of your relationship with God. Whatever the product, a successful spot makes people ACT NOW!

Creating a promotional campaign

I was part of the team that produced a major commercial campaign entitled *"Discover the Champion in You,"* for Pastor Joel Osteen, at the beginning of his role as pastor of Lakewood Church in Houston.

Here is some insight into how a major promotional campaign of this type was created, with a list of some of the most important steps in the process:

1) Assemble a great team. Pastor Osteen isn't afraid to work with people who understand and value quality and he brought together all the talent necessary to develop a successful campaign. As you create advertising for your church or ministry, you'll discover some employees have good hearts, others have good testimonies, and still others have hard-luck stories. We love all those individuals, but for breakthrough projects you also have to hire qualified and experienced people who understand creative thinking.

2) Learn the power of brainstorming. I wrote and directed the campaign only after an intense day sitting with Joel and the creative team exploring many different options. I've discovered that few ministry organizations really understand the power of brainstorming and the incredible results it can yield. If you can eliminate negative thinking, criticism, premature idea editing, and ego from a brainstorming session, the ideas generated will amaze you.

3) Make a commitment to a quality product. Few would argue that the Lakewood Church television program is one of the best looking programs on television. People seem fascinated that the Lakewood congregation, led by Pastor Osteen, grew so quickly that it moved into an 18,000-seat facility in downtown Houston. Yet, producing quality doesn't necessarily require the financial resources of a church the size of Lakewood. Quality is seldom cheap, but a dedication to excellence is more of a deciding factor than money.

4) Understand the culture you are attempting to reach. Today, popular culture is the heartbeat of this country. As I mentioned earlier, the Apostle Paul understood the power of culture when he approached the philosophers at Mars Hill. He could have said: "I'm going to preach the message of the Gospel no matter what." He didn't do that. He respected his audience's culture, values, and ideas. And once he had won their respect, he was able to reach them in a far deeper way.

As of this writing, I've worked with Joel Osteen and Lakewood Church for 20 years. During that time, I've noticed that they are constantly changing, updating, and growing. With every effort, they attempt to exceed their last program, and they never feel they've "arrived."

Don't make your goal "success;" make it "growth." Leadership expert John Maxwell counsels that once you succeed at something, your task is over, and you begin to stagnate. But if your goal is growth you never stop learning, trying new options, and increasing.

Direct Response Advertising

In the past, the advertising world was simple. You create a commercial or print ad, send it to a radio, TV station or magazine, and then see what happens.

No matter how great the advertising there was never a way to establish a direct link between the advertising and eventual sales.

Then one day media people woke up to "direct-response advertising," which took the form of infomercials, toll-free phone numbers, outbound telemarketing, and more. Next, research invaded, and suddenly we were thrown into focus groups and surveys – and now we receive a steady stream of research questionnaires on an endless variety of subjects.

It's becoming confusing and complex. Most of my clients have little idea of the difference between the various types of advertising available to us today.

Most people don't realize that the infomercial industry was born because smaller companies couldn't afford to do major advertising campaigns and needed results right away.

Madison Avenue advertising legend David Ogilvy started using direct response when a small hotel owner wanted to advertise but had an incredibly small budget. Ogilvy invested his client's small budget into cheap penny postcards, and a few weeks later, the hotel was full.

His most famous quote was: "For 40 years I have been a voice crying in the wilderness, trying to get my fellow advertising practitioners to take direct response seriously. Direct response was my first love, and later, my secret weapon."

As I said earlier in this chapter, the goal of direct response is to get the audience to respond now – immediately.

So whether one uses penny postcards, brochures, radio spots, Internet sites, or a million other advertising methods, the key is response. Remember, your audience has no idea that you need support or want them to act, unless you tell them – and give them a way to respond.

Whether we like to admit it or not, nearly every Christian media professional has produced one of those dreaded "infomercials," similar to the late-night programs that sell everything from miracle bald spot reducers, to anti-cellulite cream.

Anytime you've offered a book, tape, or other product with a toll free phone number, you've used what we call "Direct Response Advertising."

To best get that "direct" response, here are the critical keys to successful direct response advertising:

1) Direct response works in multiple formats. Most of us immediately think of TV infomercials: Popiel's Pocket Fisherman, Ginsu Knives, the George Foreman Grill, The Ab Blaster, or miracle tools or personal care products. Actually, direct response works extremely well in print and on radio too. Direct response is simply presenting a product or service, and then putting up a phone number and/or web site to encourage people to contact you immediately. You can do it in print and radio, and do it far cheaper in those media, so don't forget those alternatives when thinking of direct response.

2) Testimonies are the focal point of an effective direct response campaign. I've discovered that the audience can hear a program host talk until he or she is blue in the face, but when they see the testimony of someone whose life was changed because of the product, that's when they decide, "Wow! If it works for that guy, maybe it can work for me." (Are you paying attention, pastors, evangelists, and Christian program hosts?)

We know that phone calls generally spike up during testimonies, because that's when it hits home to people, and they respond. So whether it's a secular infomercial and they see a housewife use the George Foreman Grill effectively, and they think "If it's that easy for her, then I'm going to order it." Or, whether it's a Christian program, testimonies are absolutely critical. So begin by searching your partner letters, testimonies, or interviewing people in your church or ministry – you could even have a little booth in the back of your church announcing, "If this church or ministry has made an impact on you or someone you know tell us about it." Interview these people and put them on your program, because it will make a huge impact on your media outreach. Testimonies are critical.

3) Demonstration is vital: People want to see how a product or service works, and that's why all the secular infomercials on TV demonstrate their product. Does the gospel work? Does salvation work? Can people's lives really be transformed? Let's demonstrate it. If there's any way you can demonstrate the pastor's teaching and how it works for people, do it. Does your message work in the office?

School? During a crisis? During times of depression? Demonstration is absolutely important, and has a dramatic impact on the audience.

4) Length is important. Unless your product or service is already known by everyone watching the program, I don't recommend a 30-second DR spot. Frankly, you have to get the viewer off the sofa and over to the phone, then get him or her to write down the number and call. You simply can't do that in 30 seconds. My personal recommendation is to produce spots of 60 seconds or more. About half of what I create are sixty-second to two-minute ads. I've discovered that you need that time to demonstrate the product, service, or message, edit in a short testimony and give the audience the opportunity to respond.

In image advertising, McDonald's, Nike, FedEx, or other companies like those, make image work in 30 seconds because they're just trying to reinforce an existing good image.

In DR, you want the audience to <u>act</u>. So don't be afraid to stretch out your approach.

5) Use long-form direct response: Basically, I decide to make a 30-minute program when the product, service, or message is something that needs extensive explanation – if it's a complex concept. But in those cases, don't forget that people are tuning in and out of your program every seven to nine minutes (which is true for any program). Therefore, most half-hour infomercials are not really 30-minute shows, but they are three, seven to nine minute shows. You use the shorter segments because you want to make sure to demonstrate the product, show a testimony, and give people an opportunity to order during each segment.

In fact, one of the major principles I teach my clients is that if you're not doing a product spot later in the program, you're missing a huge number of people who are not going to be there at the end of the show. Likewise, if you're not offering it in the middle of the program - you're missing a lot of people who weren't there at the beginning and won't be there at the end.

My best advice?

Keep in mind that your audience is not a lake; it's a stream - constantly changing and constantly moving.

6) Direct response needs to be hip and contemporary. Make it cool, and make it look good. Like I said before – you don't have to be cheesy and cornball to be successful at direct response. Today, companies like Kodak, Panasonic, Sony, and Pennzoil are producing infomercials and taking them to a whole different level. Remember Ginsu knives: "The miracle knife that cuts through a can?"

They were cheesy back then.

But now they're creating a new generation of infomercials that look more like an episodic drama. There's no hard-sell. It's more dramatic, and the audience gets caught up because of the story, but the ultimate goal is still to sell those knives.

Recently, our company produced a direct response spot for Joyce Meyer Ministries, based on Joyce's book "Beauty from Ashes," published by Time Warner. It was very contemporary. We used photos of Joyce as a young woman, and told the story of her early abuse and failure, and how God redeemed and restored her life.

With help from the spot, the book began selling so fast that the publisher had trouble keeping up with the printing, and they're the largest publisher in America. It was a very high-quality spot, drove the audience to the toll-free number and to the website, and we were very proud of our creative approach.

So direct response advertising can look and sound as good as anything on radio or television.

Remember that direct response advertising can be very effective, when you use the right principles and techniques to get the audience's attention, and get them to act.

Reality Advertising

In this arena it's all about what's real. Advertising teacher Roy Williams (wizardacademy.com) has been writing for some time about the explosion of reality programming. Reality TV is certainly not new, following hot on the heels of what he calls the "Fantasy Adventure" fad in programming and advertising that reached a peak in the eighties. A year ago I would have predicted the certain death of reality programs, but I have to admit, their staying power is amazing. Surviving on islands, finding a new wife for dad, challenging obstacles and horrors, seeking wives and husbands, living in houses with Tammy Faye and porn stars, the flood of bizarre reality concepts continues unabated.

But now, Williams is preaching the gospel of reality <u>advertising</u>, as the trend in reality programming has trickled down into the commercials that surround the programs. Certainly, as a commercial director, I've seen a strong increase in clients wanting to portray real people instead of actors, less gloss and hype, and more "real-life" situations in spots.

So, as faith-based producers, how can we maximize the trend in reality advertising to the commercials we create for our programs, products, and services? Here are some thoughts and ideas as you brainstorm your next advertising campaign or program:

1) Use more real people. Instead of setting up situations portrayed with actors, find real executives, flight attendants, bookstore owners, housewives, etc. Limit the pre-written scripts; let real people tell the story in their own words.

2) Don't worry about shooting and editing a perfect spot. A number of years ago, I produced and directed a series of segments for the nationwide TV broadcast of a presidential nominating convention. Major advertising agencies were of course involved, so I did my best to shoot and edit a series of flawless segments. But during the screening, the creative director of the largest ad agency said: "The segments are <u>too</u> good. If people feel they're too slick, they won't believe us. Take them back to the editing room and make them a little rough around the edges." I have to admit, that was the first time a client told me my project was "too good." So I made a few of the edits less than perfect, softened the focus on a few shots, shook the camera a little, and sure enough, the agency loved them, and they were very well received during the national broadcast. I learned an important lesson: *It's important that the audience feels you're being honest, and not pulling something over on them.*

3) In the words of Roy Williams: **"Refer to things in your ads that you know your customers have experienced."** I call this technique "using a reality hook" If your audience has experienced the situation in their personal lives, it's more likely they'll identify with your product, service or message.

Do You Really Understand Your Client's Vision?

Remember the key to any successful media campaign is the client's vision. In the ministry world, the "client" is often a pastor, evangelist, or ministry leader. Perhaps you're working on a TV commercial with a client, or perhaps a training video or religious program for a pastor or ministry leader. Whatever your situation, to produce a successful program or spot, you have to completely understand your client's vision and goals for the project.

I recently arranged for a television producer to interview for a position as head of the media department at a major organization. After the interview, that producer called me and said, in a rather upset voice: "I was interested in a job opportunity, but they wanted me to sign on for their vision." He was not happy, and as a result, turned down the job. My response to the producer was the exact opposite of what he expected. I told him that "signing on to a client's vision" is the critical first step in any project we undertake. In fact, if a potential client doesn't have a vision for what they want to accomplish, then I'm not interested in working with them.

There are media producers who have worked with clients, bosses, pastors, executives, and other leaders for years, yet have never really understood their vision and goals. Therefore, their programs never reach their potential. How do you do it? Here are a few simple ways:

Before you begin a project, sit down with the executive, agency, ministry leader, investor, or client and ask direct questions about why he or she is doing what they are doing, what he or she hopes to achieve, what their motivations are, and how they'll measure success. Don't be embarrassed. They're asking you to be the media gate-keeper to a massive audience. If you don't have all the answers, and you try to act like you do, you'll be cheating everyone involved.

Read anything you can get your hands on about the client. Books, teaching tapes, magazine or newspaper articles, bio information —anything that will tell you his or her history, background, areas of expertise, etc. Talk to friends and get their impressions and learn from their experiences with the client. The very first step I take once I decide to work with a client is to have them send me a box full of books, teaching tapes, sermons, and printed material about the pastor. I want to get inside his or her head and completely understand their vision. I sometimes take two or three months researching this information before I actually do any media work for the client.

Decide ahead of time if this is something you can commit to with passion and excitement. You won't succeed in a project in which you don't believe. Perhaps you don't like the product or message, perhaps the chemistry just isn't right with the client, or perhaps you find integrity or character problems. Whatever it might be, if it keeps you from approaching the project with enthusiasm, then don't waste your time.

Finally, remember it's not just a job, it's a vision. As the Bible says: "Without a vision, the people perish." It's no different in the media.

Chapter 3

Finding the Right Team

—ɯ—

Most pastors, evangelists, and ministry leaders have a vision for media, but aren't sure how to make that vision happen. I can state emphatically that the foundation of any media success is hiring the right team to create, shape, and lead any media outreach. I recently heard T.D. Jakes preach a message to pastors on the importance of Moses' staff, and the correlation with our administrative staffs today. Among other things, Jakes said that God instructed Moses to never do anything without his staff, understand its importance, and know that God would work miracles for the Israelites through Moses' staff.

Not a bad parallel.

In most cases when an organization is floundering, it's because the wrong leader or staff has been hired. Troubled ministries are usually in the hands of someone currently incapable of building an outreach to match the organization's vision. To keep that from happening in *your* ministry, use this simple guide to help you find the right person, at the right experience and salary level, to make your media ministry a success.

When it comes to media, your major hiring choices come on three levels:

1) The "techie" person. This employee can be either a part-time freelancer or a fulltime employee. Salary range: low. *Experience*: Little to none. Sometimes, just a passion for electronics is enough.

Occasionally this person comes to the ministry from a local radio or TV station. *Expertise*: A "techie" generally knows a little about video and/or audio, can shoot with a video camera, do simple editing, and set up video screens, projectors, and audio gear. This is an important person on your team, because he or she knows a little about a lot of different things, but generally isn't a real expert at anything. His or her all-around knowledge can come in handy. *Best Use*: Helping you get started on a local basis. If you have a low budget, this person is probably your best bet. You can pay him or her on a part time or freelance basis, or per project. If the person's a church member, better yet. Perhaps they could do the work on a volunteer basis as part of their personal ministry.

But if you have a regional or national goal for your media outreach, don't expect a "techie" to be able to handle your needs. You'll need a more experienced producer. For that, I would recommend you hire:

2) A church or ministry Media Director. *Employment:* Usually a fulltime employee, but occasionally can be freelance, depending on the production level. Salary range: Medium to high, depending on resume. *Experience*: Five to 10 years minimum. *Expertise*: A church/ministry media director should have a background in television production. But these professionals are most often generalists, so they can do a little bit of everything. This is important for a young media outreach. They occasionally come from audio backgrounds. *Best Use*: This category covers a wide range of good media directors, which could include a local professional in your church community, but could also include the media directors at the largest church and ministry programs in the country. The more experience they have, the better for you. They should be able to coordinate a broad media outreach, including radio, TV, and the Internet. The quality and production value of your program will dictate the level of experience you'll need in your media director, and the best ones are worth every penny.

But don't expect him or her to have a strong outside perspective from working with top media ministries. If you plan to re-brand your media outreach, or are looking to establish a national or global outreach, then I would also suggest a:

3) Media consultant. *Employment*: Consultant basis, either on a monthly retainer or per project. This is the most expensive option, but if you're serious, this is an important step. *Experience*: A great deal. This person should have a strong track record working with national churches and ministries. Consultants should be able to apply their experience to your outreach. *Expertise*: The right consultant will be able to work in many areas of media ministry and will have much broader expertise in specialties such as production, direct response, program syndication, creativity, strategic planning, and more. Another important advantage of a media consultant is access to industry contacts. They will have extensive relationships in ministry support areas like direct mail marketing, media buying, fulfillment, lighting, equipment dealers, set designers, etc.

Special Note: The best media consultants don't take the place of your full-time media director, but come alongside your ministry to give you an outside perspective, create a new look and style for your program, enhancing your marketing and audience response, and more. Media consultants often have numerous clients, allowing them to bring a wide range of experience to your program. So don't let your fulltime staff feel intimidated or insecure when you bring a media consultant to the table. On the contrary, impress on them the opportunity to expand their experience, knowledge, and possibilities while the consultant is available. Your media director working with the right consultant can be a powerful combination for the success of your ministry.

One issue that robs churches and ministries of a greater impact is the myth that all consultants are out to "rip off" the church or ministry. For some reason, this belief is widely accepted. Certainly some churches and ministries have hired incompetent consultants, but in most cases, the pastor didn't do his homework, and made a bad hiring decision. There are bad consultants just like there are bad employees.

But the truth is, quite often, the best people have no desire to work full time for a single church or ministry. They have enormous expertise, and would rather move from ministry to ministry and make a difference on a much larger scale.

And to not benefit from that kind of expertise is foolish.

The next time one of your administrators or staff tries to tell you all consultants are a mistake, ask them for examples. Chances are, they're just repeating the well worn myth they heard from someone else.

Certainly you should evaluate the consultant's track record and qualifications, but if you want the best financial, media, building, strategic planning, or administrative advice – very often, a consultant is the right answer. A little later in the book, I'll give you some powerful ideas for making your consulting relationships work more effectively.

In Praise of Disagreement

The Key to unlocking openness at work is to teach people to give up having to be in agreement. We think agreement is so important. Who cares? You have to bring paradoxes, conflicts, and dilemmas out in the open, so collectively we can be more intelligent than we can be individually.

—Peter Senge

Before we go any further, I want to say something about working with your team. One of the most awkward and difficult areas I've encountered within churches and ministries is dealing with conflict and disagreement.

I say let's hear it for creative conflict. Today, in this strange era where tolerance is held up as the highest good, people think that we, as Rodney King said, "just have to get along." But the fact is, some choices are better than others, some ideas are stronger, and some outcomes more successful.

And yet, one of the greatest obstacles to growth in churches and ministries across the country is the misdirected need for everyone to agree. Over and over, I encounter employees with great ideas, terrified to disagree with the pastor or ministry leader, thinking that conflict will somehow be translated as disloyalty.

But the secret to breakthrough thinking and powerful change is that unique mix of ideas that generates creative sparks. Remember that conflict isn't strife.

There's no question that strife can be the most devastating virus to exist in an organization. Strife creates bitterness, resentment, and fosters disaster. Churches have split, and effective ministries have collapsed because someone allowed the seeds of strife to grow out of control.

But positive disagreement is the catalyst that explodes into original thinking. Proverbs 27:17 says: *"As iron sharpens iron, so one man sharpens another."* And that doesn't happen unless the two pieces of iron run into each other.

The lesson? Don't be afraid of conflicting ideas.

How can you use positive conflict to your advantage? Here are some suggestions:

1) Create an atmosphere where innovation and creativity are welcomed and even rewarded. Too many churches and ministries are locked into what worked in the past. Change is here whether you like it or not, and yesterday's ideas won't solve today's challenges.

2) Reward creative employees. Yes, we want to appreciate and love everyone on an equal basis. But the fact is, not every staff member brings the same value to your organization. Reward the innovative thinkers. Napoleon said that men were willing to march to their deaths for a piece of ribbon on their shirt. It doesn't take much to motivate people. A little appreciation and reward goes a long way.

3) Encourage conflict without humiliation or embarrassment. Real creative meetings aren't about who's idea is best. They're about getting all the good ideas on the table. Never criticize someone's idea during a brainstorming session – no matter how bad it sounds – because they'll shut down. Who knows? That person's next idea might have been the one that saved the organization.

4) Challenge your team to worry less about conflict and more about creativity. I know of one ministry that actually printed signs for everyone's desk that said "Just Follow the Instructions." That attitude is a death blow to creativity. Start encouraging people to think differently and stop following the crowd.

5) If you make a mistake, make a big one. Fail gloriously. Mess up with flair. Shoot for the great ideas and if you fall short, get up and keep moving forward. Keep your people on a path to greatness by keeping their focus on grand possibilities and worry less about the occasional failure.

Don't feel insecure when employees or team members disagree with you or each other. As long as everyone is loyal to the organization and the mission before you, a little conflict might be just what you need to smash through the ceiling of mediocrity and find the best answers.

Catching the pastor's vision: Tips for the media director

When I consult with local churches and ministries, I'm generally faced with a frustrated local employee who's at his or her wit's end. They're usually good producers, with experience, and often have a real calling to use media to take the gospel to this culture. But in nearly every case, he or she is either burned out, upset, or ready to quit.

Ninety percent of the time, I get the same response from them: "The pastor just doesn't have a vision for television." It can also come in other laments, such as: "Every time I try something new, the pastor hates it." Or the tried and true: "The pastor just doesn't get it – he or she doesn't watch TV, so he or she doesn't understand how to use television as a tool to reach the community."

And, last but certainly not least: "I've never had the budget I really need to do the job." In the words of a former President: "I feel your pain." I've worked with enough pastors, evangelists, and ministry leaders over the last 30 years to understand these frustrations and challenges.

Over those years, I've discovered five critical steps to help you get in sync with the pastor, and hopefully give him or her better vision for the possibilities of using television to impact this generation for Christ. If you are a media ministry director trying to bring your ministry into sync, try:

1) Changing the pastor's perception of you. Convince him or her that you're not a "techie," but are instead a "PRODUCER." In most churches and ministries, the "media person" is perceived by the pastor and staff as little more than someone who can "assemble" the A/V equipment. They recognize that this person is astute at electronics. But when the pastor views his media person only as a "techie," he or she is not likely to develop a close friendship, or trust the media director with the all-important personal vision.

2) Thinking from the pastor's point of view. I've been in meetings between pastors and media staff, when all the media people talked about was wireless mics, video levels, tape formats, NLE's, and a million other technical things about which the pastor had no clue. His interest lies in words like preaching, communicating, impact, storytelling, changing lives – not linear vs. non-linear editing. Until you can get on his wavelength, he'll continue to tune you out. Make sure the pastor understands that your heart is with his vision.

3) Getting past budget battles. You work at a church – not a Hollywood studio, so get over it! Low budgets are a way of life. Instead of moping around constantly depressed and complaining about all the things you wish you had, start using what you do have more effectively. Trust me – constant beefing about how small your budget is will not endear you to the pastor or administrator. So understand that you have realistic budget limitations, and adjust.

When the pastor and administrator see how you handle a limited budget, they'll be much friendlier when the next round of funding comes through. So ease up and make the most of what you have. And if you find you just can't do that, then I suggest for your mental health that you get another job. Why be miserable for the rest of your life?

One positive way around a perpetually low budget is to get out there and raise money yourself. Independent producers do it everyday, and it works just as well for a motivated church or ministry producer. There are numerous Christian media producers around the country who have gone to local merchants, business leaders, and foundations to raise money for studios, equipment, and other needs. Do you have any idea the high esteem your pastor would place you in if you suddenly brought in enough money to expand your television ministry?

4) Becoming an "idea source" for the pastor. In many churches the pastor feels like everyone wants him to come up with all the ideas. But when you begin offering creative ideas on a regular basis, the pastor will feel that he has a real source of new concepts and inspiration. He'll more likely call you into important meetings, and listen to your advice.

But to be a successful idea source, you have to understand one important principle: *Make sure your ideas are possible.*

Work within the budget framework of the church. Don't suggest shooting the Christmas Musical in the United Kingdom with the London Symphony Orchestra, unless the church can afford it. Sure it's a terrific idea, but what's the point if you can't pay for it?

Also, work within the style and outreach of the church. If your church is in a rural area, a hip inner-city style outreach might be a wonderful idea, but not appropriate for your target audience. Always keep in mind to whom you are ministering.

And finally, work within the ministry and calling of the pastor. Every pastor has a personal style as well as an overall calling and direction for his life and ministry. To ask him to dramatically deviate from that style of ministry is like asking Kobe Bryant to enter the Olympics as a downhill skier – you're in for a lot of problems. Recognize the inherent spiritual gifts and expertise of the pastor, and use those in your creative thinking.

5) Think about the "Big Picture." Until you think of yourself on a higher level, no one else will. Learn about product "branding" and apply those principles to yourself. Increase your perception in the eyes of those around you and you'll be amazed at the new meetings and high-level decisions in which you'll be invited to participate. Your level of responsibility should rise noticeably and rapidly.

But, even if you've spent years with the pastor and staff holding you in low esteem, and know the change will come slowly, it is still worth the effort.

Working with consultants: Ten big mistakes

Today, "outsourcing" is all the rage in corporate America. The theory behind the practice is worth considering. If there is some aspect of your business that you don't do well, then outsourcing it to someone who does, makes sense. For instance, a corporation that builds computers might not be so strong at strategic planning, or a company that manufactures sports equipment, probably doesn't understand marketing and public relations. So they find consultants with experience and success in those areas to give them advice, training, and expertise.

Could churches, ministries, and other Christian organizations benefit from the concept?

Absolutely.

Although our mandate for reaching the lost couldn't be simpler, the various ways available to accomplish that mandate couldn't be more complex. Today, churches and ministries routinely use new technology, the media, marketing strategies, leadership training, and other tools to make their outreaches, educational programs, and ministries more effective.

That's why thousands of churches and para-church ministries around the world use consultants – or "experts" – in particular fields to help them understand and implement their outreaches more effectively.

Consultants are available in areas such as Christian education, computer technology, media, strategic planning, leadership, marketing and advertising, and more, and they can make a real difference in raising the level of competence for your staff members, employees, and leaders.

Instead of hiring more employees with salaries and benefits, find outside consultants with experience and success in those areas to give you advice, training, and expertise.

Today, thousands of churches and ministries around the world use consultants to help them understand and implement outreaches more effectively. However, few churches and ministries use consultants well. As a result the ministries don't achieve the substantial benefits consultants can provide.

Here's a list of the "Ten Big Mistakes" ministries make when working with consultants:

Mistake #1: Assuming you don't need a consultant. In the secular business world, consultants provide fresh perspective, and companies are willing to spend for that. Leadership expert John Maxwell calls it "fresh eyes." Everyone needs someone from the outside to bring a new perspective, valuable experience, and cutting edge thinking to their situation. If the most successful companies in America use consultants, perhaps you and your ministry should consider them as well.

Mistake #2: Bringing in a consultant before checking his or her track record. The best consultants can demonstrate a clear record of accomplishments. You can tell from past clients when consultants have what it takes to impact your church or ministry. But, don't just take the consultant's word for his or her abilities. View their demo reel, client list, portfolio, spreadsheets, or other information that document past successes. Always call the consultant's former clients. Don't just accept the consultant's list of accomplishments.

Mistake #3: Barring the consultant from access to the top person in your organization. Anyone responsible for expressing the pastor's or ministry leader's vision through media needs "face-time" with the boss. If the pastor or ministry leader is too busy to make time for the people, including the consultant, who act as his or her gatekeeper, priorities need adjusting.

Mistake #4: Having your middle managers evaluate and criticize the consultant's recommendations. Make sure upper-level people get involved in this process. Recognize that if your staff could have solved the problem, you wouldn't have needed the consultant in the first place. Christian organizations routinely hire outside experts who are constantly being micro-managed and critiqued by less experienced in-house staff, because the pastor doesn't want to get involved. Make sure that middle managers leave the consultant alone long enough to produce results.

Don't let jealousies and turf battles block any good work your consultant might do.

Mistake #5: Tying your consultant's hands financially. Sit down in advance. Create an appropriate budget, and then let the consultant work within that framework. Don't nickel and dime them, especially if they're getting results. The most successful consultants can be expensive, but if they accomplish the goal you have given them, they are worth every penny.

Mistake #6: Harboring fears that the consultant will "take over". Most consultants work with numerous clients, travel, set their own hours, and run their own businesses, so why would they want to take over your ministry? It's a baffling, but frequent concern. The consultant's greatest joy is to be wildly successful taking care of the problem they were hired to fix. They get no joy or benefit from hijacking your organization.

Mistake #7: Refusing to take your consultant seriously. I've never understood churches and ministries that hire consultants and then don't listen to them. Sometimes this is caused by insecurity, inexperience, or just plain ego. The best consultants come to you after working with some of the most successful churches, ministries, and organizations in America. Not listening to that type of expertise is like a football team not listening to a winning coach.

Mistake #8: Firing the consultant at the first mistake. Consultants need the freedom to make mistakes. It means they are trying new things, over-reaching, and pushing the limits. Give them a little latitude, and they'll pay you back with creative work, innovative ideas, and most of all – results. When they do make a mistake don't just dismiss them. Discuss the problem at length and let the consultant defend his or her strategy. Listen and you might just change your opinion – and your future.

Mistake #9: Hesitating to recommend a successful consultant to others. Every client wants to think they're the most important, and even the only client of a consultant. But remember, the more clients your consultant has, the wider his or her range of experience. More experience means more ideas to bring to your table. Although good consultants keep their information confidential, their experiences from other ministries will only help you.

Mistakes #10: Using the consultant only for short-term projects. In the secular world, client-consultant relationships work for years, and even decades. In television production, for instance, it might take years to build or re-shape a television outreach – especially at a national level. Look for a consultant that can provide a long-term plan for helping you achieve your goals. Make sure the consultant has the staff, resources, and tools to stay with you, taking your church or ministry to the far reaches of success and effectiveness.

Chapter 4

Producing Creative Content

—⁓—

For most of my career I have been making my living watching church services. Although I frequently create television and motion picture projects for secular studios, networks, and other sources, I also produce and direct television programming for a wide range of churches and ministries. That task enables me to watch hundreds of church services, religious events, and other evangelistic efforts and work with pastors, evangelists, teachers, and other ministry leaders to make programs more powerful and effective.

I'm especially fascinated watching church services, many of which are filled with believing prayer, heart-felt worship, and life-changing teaching and preaching.

But despite best efforts, many church services are still exercises in agony. Why is it that in some churches, worshipping the Creator of the universe is boring, frustrating, and sometimes a showcase for bad music, inept preaching, and poor taste?

Recently, while visiting some relatives and going to their Sunday service, the thought occurred to me that many of the techniques we use in making a Christian television program more effective would also increase the interest and participation of the local congregation as well.

I'm a "behind the scenes" guy – a teacher, consultant, and coach. My comments don't come as prophetic word. Rather, they deal with practical, everyday, but important aspects of ministry. Many of these ideas will be completely new. Others will be things you already know, but need to be reminded of.

My father is a pastor, so I remember well how he labored to increase attendance, preach a potent sermon, and create a worshipful atmosphere for the congregation. Behind the scenes, I mowed the grass, swept the floor, carried the guest speaker's luggage, copied bulletins, and even worked as backup pianist. So from earliest memory, my life has been caught up in the desire to make church more relevant and fascinating to people.

And, since so much of the content of any media ministry evolves from basic church services, as those services grow in power and relevance, the media outreach becomes more powerful.

It starts with good preaching

No mortal can bring anointing into a dead situation. But through a lifetime of watching thousands of services, I have discovered important principles that if put into practice, will allow the Holy Spirit to work more effectively. They dramatically change the way the audience reacts to any service.

But before you dismiss these ideas as "worldly science" outside the realm of the Holy Spirit, let me counter these common arguments:

1) "I don't worry about the service; I just let the Holy Spirit take over." Theoretically, that's a wonderful concept. We all hope that happens at every service. But in reality, there are important things that we need to do in preparation for the Holy Spirit to work. You wouldn't have a major operation by a Christian surgeon who preferred not to prepare for the surgery, but wanted to just let the Holy Spirit work. I'm glad he's open to the Spirit, but I also want him to have the right equipment, a trained support team, a keen understanding of my condition, and great skill.

Today's pastor, evangelist, or teacher needs no less.

2) "I just preach the old-fashioned gospel." Preaching the old-fashioned gospel is fine – using old fashioned methods isn't. If by the old fashioned gospel, you mean uncompromising preaching, anointed prayer, and powerful ministry, I'm all for it. But, be sensitive to today's needs, problems, and concerns.

3) "I don't go in for all this marketing stuff." Actually, in the advertising world, marketing can be defined as the science of positioning your product in a way most people will respond to. That's not terribly different from your job as a minister. Of course we need to draw the line at unscrupulous techniques and questionable tactics, but as much as possible we need to be developing new methods of presenting the gospel message to a hurting world in ways it will understand and receive. I don't believe in "chasing marketing" because ultimately we're communicating an eternal message, one that's outside any particular time, era, or culture. French Philosopher Simone Weil said, "To be always relevant, you have to say things that are eternal."

I think that's what "relevance" is – speaking eternal truths without regard to fashions and trends. To chase most people's idea of "relevance" is really what keeps you most irrelevant.

How to ruin a church service

With these thoughts in mind, let me introduce you to **"Phil Cooke's top ten list of ways to ruin a church service."** *(You have my permission to copy this and hang it on your bathroom mirror for future reference) The infamous steps include:*

1) Don't concern yourself with the congregation's point of view. After all, it's you who has the anointing, right? In a theater, a television studio, or on a motion picture stage, the single most important person to the success of a production is the director. The director has the creative vision for the entire project, and it is that vision that guides the writers, actors, camera people, and other crew. Most people don't know that the role of director is a fairly recent one. In fact, it was developed in the theater in Europe during the late 1800's and up until that time, the actors themselves staged the play. But, an actor finally asked, "What does the audience think?" So, it was decided that one of the actors would sit in the audience watching the rehearsal and make comments based on how he would react as a member of the audience.

Thus, the role of "director" was born to provide a person <u>to</u> <u>represent the audience</u>. Since that time, nearly every commercial, play, TV program, or film has had a director – to stand back and shape the presentation from the perspective of the audience.

We could do well to learn from that tradition. How long has it been since you went out and just sat in a pew? (Not from the front row, but say, 15 to 20 rows back). How is the lighting? How is the music? How loud is the speaker system? Is the pulpit area appealing? Do the flowers and/or plants get in the way? Are there other physical distractions?

But there's more to it. How often do you really try to identify with the needs, hopes and dreams of those in your congregation? I know pastors who are "escorted" on stage to preach, and then "escorted" off stage to their waiting private garage. They never shake anyone's hands, hear their hurts, or feel their hugs.

Small church or large – don't lose touch with the perspective of the people sitting in the seats.

2) Never tell stories – just preach the Word. Want to put people to sleep? Don't tell a story. As I've said before, this Sunday, preachers all across America will preach sermons without telling a single story. In every case, it will be a mechanical, dry, and boring exercise.

Look at the ministry of Jesus. Storytelling was about all he did. He put the most profound and deep concepts into simple and compelling stories that captivated people and changed their lives. As a kid, I listened for hours to my dad's stories of fighting in World War II, and I have watched great preachers hold thousands in rapt attention with a powerful story.

Through the centuries, the power of a story has held generations captive, and it's curious that instead of the Bible being a book of theological arguments and lessons, it's generally a book of stories.

You'll never preach an effective sermon without using the power of stories.

3) Become obsessed with "special music." What, no choir number today? Pastors, stay with me. The success of your Sunday service doesn't depend on having "special music." Look at the competition you face. Everyday, the members of your church can turn on a local Christian radio or television station and hear the finest music the Christian world has to offer. So let's face it, when they hear Brother Ralph and Sister Glenda singing "The Church Triumphant" on Sunday morning, they'll be weeping alright – but not for joy.

And, don't feel you have to have a choir number each week either. I'm reminded of Joel Osteen's father, the late John Osteen at Lakewood Church in Houston. Although he was pastor of one of the great churches in America, he went years with no choir! Why? He wanted to wait until he was sure he had a choir that was <u>both</u> musically qualified and Spirit led, that would make a positive and anointed impact on the service.

Music is a wonderful tool, but don't let it make you a slave.

4) Don't question anything – keep doing the same old stuff. Why do you take up the offering the same way each week? Why do you always sing the same hymn of invitation? Why do you always make announcements? Why... why... why?

Have a solid reason for every single thing you do during a typical service. "We've always done it that way" doesn't count!

5) Use the same pulpit jokes over and over. If they laughed once they'll laugh again, right?

How about that old gem: *"I like the King James Version – if it was good enough for Paul, it's good enough for me!"*

Or, *"How many of you would rather be here than the finest hospital in town?"*

Please... please... please... find some new jokes. Your congregation is starting to laugh out of pity... not from humor.

6) The old sermons are the best. I don't need new material. Evangelists are especially guilty of this one. It used to be that since an evangelist traveled around the country, he could preach the same sermons and tell the same stories over and over and it wouldn't matter. The audience was always changing. But now that television and radio have entered the picture, that's no longer true.

The headlines, issues, and problems we face are constantly changing, and our sermons should be developing too. The message of the gospel never changes, but the way we present it should be updated and strengthened.

I would especially caution against using "sugar sticks" – those old standby messages that you can pull out of your pocket at the drop of a hat. (You know the ones – the sermons that will always get a rise out of the audience or get the phones ringing during telethons). The danger here is that the more you preach the same sermon, the more difficult it is to preach it with conviction, originality, and excitement.

Although new material may be unproven and a little shaky, there's a wonderful spontaneity and excitement about breaking new ground.

7) Dismiss the surrounding culture – I hate their music and movies anyway. Jesus always understood the culture that surrounded his ministry. He framed powerful sermons with stories that were filled with cultural and social perspective. Your messages will always be more effective when you tie your points to issues that your audience is facing everyday – drugs, abuse, AIDS, finances, family issues, violence, etc.

8) I don't know much about this audience – So what? They're just people. All the same, right?
Don't take for granted that everyone you're preaching to is your age, comes from your background, or has your interests. Of course you *know* they're not, but how often do you actually wonder about how a child will understand the message, or a teen, or a senior? Demographics is the science of understanding everything you can about your audience – their ages, their backgrounds, their habits, their needs, etc.

Madison Avenue spends billions of dollars each year tailoring ad messages to every age group. Make sure you're targeting your audience in a similar way.

9) I've stopped learning – All I need is a pulpit and a Bible. Believe it or not, I actually had a pastor friend recently give me the worn out adage, "I'm glad I never went to cemetery... oh, I mean seminary." There are still pastors, evangelists, teachers, and Christian leaders who believe higher learning is for snobs, elites, and those not concerned about "real ministry." Nothing could be further from the truth, especially during this period when there are wonderfully anointed Christian colleges, Bible schools, and training centers all across the United States and the world.

I've always valued the energy and passion of those who had a dramatic conversion experience and felt called directly into the ministry. But now, when the battle for Truth is more desperate than ever, we need to know how to defend our calling at every level, and have the academic background to avoid theological error and ministry mistakes.

We'll never make an impact on our society without brilliant men and women who can preach the message of the gospel and answer the world's questions with intelligence, authority, and compassion.

Take the time to find a good Christian school and get the training you need, no matter how late in life you start. And don't go to a diploma mill for convenience just to have a diploma hanging on the wall.

10) Never be open to the Spirit – stay with the bulletin. As you can tell by now, this is not an excuse to skip your homework. I've worked with too many people who failed to study and prepare on the hope that the Holy Spirit would show up and do their work for them. When you talk with the really gifted and anointed pastors, evangelists, and teachers out there, you'll find that although God works in sovereign ways, He will honor preparation.

Many television and film directors refuse to do their homework because they prefer to rely on the "spontaneity of the moment." But what happens when they arrive on the studio set and that spontaneity doesn't happen? I always believe in having a map, and if I get a creative spark on the set, that's wonderful. But if not, I can always fall back on my original plan.

Prepare your message the same way. If God shows up (and I hope he does) toss your plan and flow in that Spirit. But just in case He decides to work through your preparation, be sure you have something well planned.

Constantly remind yourself that ministering to people is the art of understanding the fine line between speaking the Word in boldness, and being sensitive to the needs and hurts of your audience.

There's a time for each, but effective ministry is more often a delicate combination of both.

And finally, keep looking at those faces out there.

Learn to distinguish between the Holy Spirit breaking hearts as a result of <u>His</u> work, and faces contorted in agony as a result of <u>your</u> work!

Confidence and Humility

I think it's time for pastors and media ministries to take a break from sending out messages on positive thinking, prosperity, confidence, self esteem, and anything else particularly uplifting for that matter.

No, I'm not crazy. I know what the Bible says about being more than conquerors, prospering Abraham, pouring out a blessing, and more. Oral Roberts – one of the most gifted preachers of our time – coined the phrase "Expect a Miracle" nearly half a century ago, but hundreds of other preachers later, we've created a Christian community where significant numbers of people think they can accomplish anything as long as they feel good about themselves, have plenty of confidence, and believe in their potential.

In the secular world, it's already well documented how public schools' focus on self-esteem during the last few decades has seriously hurt a generation of young people. Today, students care less about what they actually accomplish in school, and more about how they "feel" about it. In a major study comparing math skills among students in eight nations, Americans ranked lowest in overall competence and Koreans highest. But when researchers asked the students how good they thought they were at math, the results were exactly opposite: Americans felt they scored highest, Koreans lowest.

American students can't add, but apparently it doesn't matter as long as they feel good about themselves while they err.

Our culture has enthusiastically embraced self-esteem and personal confidence despite little real evidence that those things actually help. Psychologists Roy Baumeister and Martin Seligman suggest that more often, unusually high self-esteem is a sign of negative behavior, the type found in high profile criminals.

It's not that different in a community of Christian believers who think all we need for success is to believe in our potential. In that world, we can forget education, training, and skill, because what we believe is far more important than what we actually accomplish.

As a Christian who is a television producer in Hollywood, I regularly receive movie scripts from hopeful believers eager to break into the film business. The problem is the vast majority of the scripts are from Christians who have never learned to actually write. But when I point out the multitude of problems and mistakes in script structure, storytelling, or even grammar – I usually get the response, "God told me to write it, so I'm not interested in changing anything, or taking the time to learn."

Ah, the deceptive power of overconfidence.

If your financial planning consists solely of giving money to TV ministries and expecting God to send you a "hundred-fold return," chances are that your retirement years are going to be tough.

Yes, God does bless His people, and I financially support church and ministry outreaches, and confidence is a wonderful thing. He calls us to great things, and offers us a fulfilling role in His plan for this generation. But, He also honors preparation, discernment, knowledge, skill, and training for the task ahead.

In Exodus 31, God spoke to Moses about an artist named Bezalel. He said, "I have filled him with the Spirit of God, with skill, ability and knowledge in all kinds of crafts." God wasn't interested in hiring well meaning but incompetent people to build His temple. He wanted the best.

Real confidence and self-esteem come from actual accomplishment. Doing a job well, and gaining the respect of your boss, your friends, and your family.

Today, if we're going to make an impact in this culture for the gospel, we need to go far beyond self-esteem, good intentions, and confidence. We need intelligence, wisdom, and skill – that produces the kind of excellent work that stops the world in its tracks, and makes people want to know more about the God we worship.

Top management consultant Jay Kurtz argues: "The most dangerous person in corporate America is the highly enthusiastic incompetent. He's running faster in the wrong direction, doing horribly counterproductive things with winning enthusiasm."

Perhaps even more than competence, we as Christians need a giant dose of humility.

Humility is the great compass of life that makes sure we're prepared for the journey, gives us insight, and corrects our course. Humility reminds us that from God's perspective, over-confidence and self-esteem make no blip on His radar.

We are not "all things." We are "all things through Christ."

Until we temper our confidence with humility, all the positive thinking in the world is just a "sounding brass and a tinkling cymbal."

And the last thing the world needs is more huge egos and more lousy music.

Find inspiration in disaster

During the day of September 11th, 2001, after the terrorist attacks took place at the World Trade Center and the Pentagon, I had the opportunity to encourage Christian television and radio stations across the country to break into their regularly scheduled programming and go LIVE with programs and information related to the national crisis. It started with a single memo containing crisis programming suggestions to my media clients, but grew into something much larger, as numerous Christian stations and networks began circulating it and using it as a guideline for their producers.

Within an hour of the first airline crash, I sent a memo to about 30 of our Christian clients and associates nationwide. In the past, Christian TV and radio stations have been slow to deal with immediate issues. I've often been frustrated that while a national tragedy unfolds on secular networks, Christian stations tend to do "business as usual" and ignore these issues. But on that day, it completely changed. We saw literally hundreds of Christian television and radio stations respond with answers, encouragement, and most of all, hope.

But can a local church program have an impact in these situations? Especially since most aren't live, and must wait a few days to a week to broadcast their next program?

Absolutely.

On 9/11, I heard from numerous clients and friends who were preparing a special Sunday program to specifically deal with the crisis. Some taped it during their Wednesday night service, others taped it during a special service they conducted on Tuesday, and still others did a special studio taping.

The memo I sent to Christian stations, program producers, and churches was the following:

MEMO TO CHRISTIAN MEDIA PRODUCERS:

From a programming perspective, I would urge you to go on the air immediately if possible with content related to today's events in New York and Washington. Today and tonight, millions of people are at their television sets looking for answers. This is not the time to run "Christian TV as usual" – we need to provide answers to people filled with questions. Here are some suggestions from the team at Cooke Pictures:

1) I would suggest you go on the air immediately – tonight at the latest – with a special program of prayer, interviews, and discussions about what is happening.

2) If possible, try to connect with people well-versed in these types of events – prophecy experts, terrorism experts, college professors respected in current events and world affairs, pastors with a global perspective, or expertise on the Middle East. If you can't get them into the studio, connect with them via phone.

3) Most Christian broadcasters are not necessarily news experts and cannot compete with CNN, ABC, Fox, and others. However, we can provide spiritual insight to millions who are searching. The major networks can only repeat the facts surrounding the incidents of today so many times. Sooner or later, people will be looking for something deeper – some type of explanation, understanding, and perspective. This is an opportunity for you as a Christian broadcaster to provide that insight.

4) Stay away from "pat" answers. Chances are, more non-Christians will be watching you over the next few days than ever before. So stay away from Christian "lingo" they won't understand, and try to provide real answers to the real questions they are facing.

5) Do not be afraid to break into your regularly scheduled programming. This is the time to act, and make a real difference for the gospel.

The next day, I heard from producers at local Christian TV and radio stations who had actually been on the air with cell phone calls to people they knew in the World Trade Center. One major Christian TV station called and said they had stopped all production and had a staff conference focused on the memo, and would be changing their programming for the next two weeks in response. After receiving nearly 100 emails, the next day I followed up the first memo with the following, which I called "Crisis Programming Memo #2":

"I'm very impressed and encouraged by the numbers of stations and networks who broadcast live yesterday with up-to-the-minute reports, encouragement, spiritual help, and other information for your viewers. I think you'll find that more non-Christians are watching, so this is a great time to minister to them, as well as increase your exposure in your particular market.

As a follow up to yesterday's memo – here are some new suggestions, now that the immediate crisis is over:

1) Begin a plan for thoughtful long-term programming. Yesterday had lots of questions: "Who did it?" "Why?" "How did it happen?" Now, the facts are beginning to emerge, so be careful and don't contribute to misinformation or inaccurate reporting. Start thinking about programs related to "What do we do next?" "How can we pray for our Country now?" "How do Christians respond in times of crisis?" "What does the Bible say about national issues?" etc.

2) What is your LOCAL area doing in the wake of the crisis? A producer in Texas spent yesterday doing video reports at the local blood bank. He also did a phone interview with a local viewer's nephew who had been on the 17th floor of the World Trade Center. There are many local stories such as price gouging, airports closed, and other issues. Not to mention all the local church services, and spiritual events surrounding the crisis. Be a local spiritual voice for your audience.

3) Television programs – use your "bug". The "bug" is your logo inserted in the corner of the screen. Since more people than ever are changing channels looking for coverage, a "bug" instantly reminds them of who you are, and helps them find you in the future. Always remind your viewers of your station and how to contact you for more information.

4) The L.A. Times reports today that the secular networks have made the unprecedented decision to share all video feeds. I don't know if this extends to local stations, but check with your legal representation to find out if you could have access to this footage as well. Remember, we don't have to look like CNN, but a few shots here and there can help visualize the crisis and explain certain issues more effectively.

5) Check the NRB Website Press Release page for satellite coordinates and schedules from the major Christian networks like Lesea, TLN, CBN, and others. Local stations can use these resources when you can't afford to do your own coverage.

6) The National Religious Broadcasters organization is also posting resources from other media ministries, such as potential guest interviews, experts in certain areas, etc... Make use of these resources. If you can't fly someone in, perhaps you can do a phone interview. They'll often do whatever you need. Make it a "win-win" situation for both of you.

7) Call or email Christian stations or networks you admire for advice in situations like this. From programming suggestions to production advice, we're all in this together, so let's share information and ideas.

8) Finally – remember, this event will not be over in a day or so. The spiritual and psychological effects of a tragedy like this will linger for weeks and months to come. As horrible as it was, Oklahoma City was small compared to this, so focus on providing information and answers for the long haul. This is a remarkable chance to present spiritual answers to your audience at a time when they welcome anything you have to offer.

You have their attention. Now let's give them something to change their lives."

What started as a simple idea, in a matter of days blossomed into a remarkable event for millions of television viewers and radio listeners who had the opportunity to hear a Christian perspective on the tragic events. Within a week, church programs followed with their own original programs focused on the crisis.

If we're going to impact this culture for the gospel, we have to speak in a language and style they understand. That happened on hundreds of Christian radio and television stations across the country that week, and the results were incredible.

Chapter 5

The Technology Monster

—ᵐ—

*W*hat *do you do when you don't know what to do?* It's an important question. In today's world of television, video, audio, computers, websites, personal digital assistants and players, and the growing world of technology, every pastor, evangelist, teacher, church administrator, and audio-visual staff member is constantly faced with this important and often horrifying question.

Today it's just not enough to be a competent pastor, teacher, counselor, minister of music, or administrator. Today church and ministry leaders are faced with the nearly impossible task of not only *having expertise in their chosen field, but mastering the art of new technologies as well.*

After all, most churches or ministries would benefit from today's advances in computers, video, sound or lighting, in either their presentation of the gospel, or the multitude of administrative tasks that surround those ministries.

I'll never forget, as a preacher's kid in the 1950s and 1960s, when my father made the change from recording his sermons on bulky and hard-to-operate reel-to-reel audiotape, and began using smaller audiocassettes. As the person stuck with sitting in the little booth in the back of the church, ineptly operating the recording machines, I was thrilled with the change. It took awhile to figure it all out, but soon all I had to do was pop in a cassette and we were off and running.

We thought that audiocassettes had ushered in the space age. In reality that change was incredibly easy compared to the one church and ministry leaders are facing today. With the advent of inexpensive lighting, sound, and video technologies, nearly any church can have professional quality sound and lighting, and many are in a position to move into television and video as well. And with the advances in design and digital technology, the presentation possibilities are endless.

But, questions remain:

How do I make these changes? Where should I start? How much will it cost? Where can I get the best advice? These are questions I hear constantly.

Are you a pastor or evangelist pacing the floor late at night, watching Christian television and thinking: "I can do that"? Are you a teacher who's wondering how these new technologies can impact and improve your message? Or perhaps you're a church administrator who's wondering if your church or ministry can really afford to take the chance to move into a media ministry. Or, perhaps you are a church or ministry audiovisual staff member who's trying to find the perfect equipment mix? For all the above and more, there is hope.

And the good news is you don't have to be a trained engineer, designer, or computer expert to move into the new technologies – lighting, audio, music, video, broadcast television, computer technology, interactive websites, etc. You can find something that is both realistic and affordable for your church or outreach.

I'm a television producer, not an engineer. I'm interested in the *creative* aspects of technology – how it will effect my message, how much it will cost, and most important, how my media audience will receive that message.

We'll leave the gigahertz, lumens, and scan lines to other books, and for our purposes here, start with one of the most misunderstood aspects of technology:

"State of the Art"

The term *state-of-the-art* is thrown around in radio and television more than in any other as much as any other field. I feel sure you've heard it. Ideally, this term means that a piece of equipment *is the latest and most technologically superior item on the market.* In reality, this judgment is in the eyes of the beholder. "Experts" can and do disagree on the value of brands and technologies.

Chances are, just about every sales presentation you hear will make some reference to *state of the art.* Everyone wants to believe his or her equipment is exactly that, and in fact, many pastors and church leaders love to refer to their own lighting, sound, computer, or video equipment in just that way. Therefore, it's vitally important that you have a realistic understanding of exactly what the term means – and doesn't mean.

First, *don't believe everything you see is state-of-the-art.* Chances are the real *state-of-the-art* is still in someone's research-and-development lab down the street.

The fact is, technology keeps improving, and it's important to stay abreast of those developments. In television and video, for instance, one of the fastest changing areas is *post-production equipment* – the equipment you use to edit a program. In the past 30 years, just about everything in the post-production arena has changed – dramatically. The quality, availability, and price are vastly more favorable. Yet even as you buy, bear in mind that *state-of-the-art today* is going to be *passé tomorrow.*

Second, *make a choice you can live with.* You will only have *state-of-the-art* equipment for a short time. You will have *workhorse* equipment for a lot longer. Your challenge is to make sure the new model you buy today will last, and that it is part of an integrated system or in a sequence of upgrades.

You'll find that companies don't reinvent the entire wheel each year, but they come up with new innovations every quarter, six months, or year. Look for something that has the potential to be upgraded for an extended life.

The four factors you should consider most strongly are:

1) The Source: Who is selling/recommending this piece of equipment? Is it a reputable source? For instance, is it an experienced producer or engineer with years of ministry and church broadcasting under his/her belt? And what are his/her credits and track record? Never forget: Christian television and video production is an art form all its own, and has very particular requirements. For instance, while there's a crossover, we don't necessarily use the same equipment in churches and ministries that is used in sports television, dramatic programming, studio programs, or news.

I counsel my clients to avoid any equipment salesman who isn't first of all interested in your program formats and production requirements. After all, how can they suggest the correct equipment if they don't know intimately how it will be used and for what purpose?

2) Service: Can I get the equipment serviced easily? Inexpensively? Can I get spare parts? What is the equipment's track record with other ministries or churches?

Although you'll always be able to get a cheaper price from knock-off brands and fringe companies, your cost savings will soon get swallowed up in down time waiting for parts and service. I prefer to buy from companies who can keep me moving forward without delays and complications.

3) Price: Most expensive isn't always best. Least expensive isn't always cheapest by the time you've repaired or replaced it a dozen times. Weigh track records of similar equipment against the price. Virtually everything is negotiable, especially if you are putting together a package of several types of equipment or are outfitting a small studio.

4) Flexibility: Will the piece of equipment be compatible with other pieces of equipment? Can it move from one location to another or does it have to be permanently installed?

With the advent of digital editing environments, it's become critically important that different pieces of equipment be able to "talk to each other." For instance, in post-production, the editing software should be talking to the audio board, the graphics workstation, and other pivotal pieces of equipment. This makes for cleaner edits, easier-to-fix programs, and precise EDL's (edit decision lists) that keep track of every element of the program.

Although such equipment doesn't have to be made by the same company (and I don't know of any company that makes everything equally well), I recommend those pieces of equipment be purchased from the top branded companies – because they all know how to work with each other.

The bottom line

Get the advice of experts. Find impartial judges, consultants, and/or advisors who can help you with proper equipment and software decisions.

Where do you find these experts? Look to other churches and ministries that you admire for their effectiveness. Talk with the pastors, administrators, television and video producers, lighting and sound people, etc. You'll be surprised at how helpful they can be. They've been exactly where you are today, and many have the scars to prove it.

Spend the money to keep yourself and your in-house advisors updated and trained. Your staff members can't help you if they don't know exactly what's out there. That's why it's so important to get your people proper training and exposure to new products and ideas. That training should also involve bringing in outside consultants, teachers, producers, programmers, etc, to hold in-house workshops for your staff and volunteers to familiarize them with current techniques and equipment.

Finally, it's important to attend trade shows to really get a grasp of the big picture. Trade shows like the National Religious Broadcasters Convention, and the National Association of Broadcasters Convention are examples of events where you'll see truly *state of the art* equipment and get a better understanding of the broad marketplace.

So why begin with the term *state-of-the-art*? Because as I travel around the country working with churches and ministries, the greatest abuses and mistakes I've seen develop from this issue. In most cases, churches thought they were buying state-of-the-art, but in actuality were not. In the worst cases, they bought lesser-quality equipment and paid far too much.

Remember: *You don't have to be a trained engineer, designer, programmer, or television producer.* You just have to know where to get the information you need to make decisions that will save your church or ministry thousands, perhaps even millions of dollars.

I once received a call from a ministry that had just purchased $650,000 in post-production equipment – and the ministry hadn't even produced one program! If its program had failed, that expense would have severely damaged the ministry's financial situation and possibly destroyed it completely. I know of another ministry that spent nearly $2 million on a facility without one conversation with an experienced Christian producer, engineer, or other qualified advisor. As a consequence, they bought equipment that was very inappropriate to the situation and today, much of it sits unused.

Why?

Because that ministry was sold on "state of the art," without realizing the importance of knowing how, where, and why the equipment would be used for particular programming and ministry needs.

At this point let me mention a situation where a "state of the art" piece of equipment was actually the worst thing to buy. I once had a client who before working with me purchased a very sophisticated (and very expensive - $250,000) video switcher that had just come off the production line. In fact, this particular piece of equipment was a new design and was the first one like it ever produced.

Sitting there in the studio, it was truly a magnificent looking unit! Tour groups coming through the facility were amazed at the sophistication, and the owner proudly told everyone how "state of the art" this new product was. The new equipment was supposed to position the ministry at the cutting edge of broadcasting.

But once the equipment was installed and paid for, the bugs were discovered.

In fact, it had so many problems that the model was scrapped by the manufacturer and never offered again. My client was left with a very expensive piece of junk. And the expense didn't end with the initial purchase. Because the ministry had paid so much for the equipment, it couldn't afford to buy another model, so it had to hire another full-time maintenance engineer just to keep that unit running.

How could that mistake be avoided?

At a national television network like NBC, CBS, or ABC, they can afford to experiment with the latest technology.

Chances are you can't.

Let other people go through the heartbreak and frustration of working bugs out of new designs and equipment. And most of all let other people go through the financial (and sometimes legal) headaches.

Should you always avoid state-of-the-art equipment?

Absolutely not. But at the same time, get the information you need to accurately evaluate its function and uses for both the present and the future. Remember, you have to get the right advice from the right consultant. Don't jump too soon, and always get the information you need to make decisions that could save your church or ministry money, while giving *your message more impact.*

Your first investment should be in state-of-the-art *people*, not equipment. The finest equipment, in the hands of an average production crew, will still produce only average programs.

On the other hand, good equipment in the hands of creative, driven people will produce powerful and effective programming for the Kingdom of God.

So, in the future when we think *"state of the art"* let's also think of new ideas, creativity, and people – not just equipment and facilities.

The World Wide Web

As I mentioned, I became a Christian through the stage door. My father was a pastor, and as long as I can remember I've worked behind the scenes sweeping floors, mowing the grass, folding church bulletins, setting chairs, and helping my father in his ministry. In those days we tried everything to draw a crowd – youth rallies, door to door witnessing, pot lucks, and more. I probably walked 100 miles when my Dad decided we should promote a revival by putting door hangers on every door in town.

Today, as a media consultant to some of the largest churches and ministries in the country, I'm still working behind the scenes – even though it's on a much larger scale. But in one ministry meeting recently, we discussed the organization's website. Looking at that site, I was reminded of that 100-mile trek putting out door hangers. That site was just a digital version of that 40-year-old door hanger idea of my father's.

If your church or ministry website isn't working for you, then you're wasting time and money. An effective Internet site is more than just a handout with address information and the times of your services. Today we live in a digital age, and people of all ages are spending more and more time online. I recently directed a 15-minute short film for a Japanese company's website. It wasn't an advertisement, and the product never showed up in the film. But the company understood the power of the Internet, and wanted an entertaining short movie to associate with their product. They're goal wasn't immediate sales, it was to build the power of their brand.

Our team at Cooke Pictures is working with an innovative new ministry to create a data bank of resources for family issues, including addiction, abuse, and divorce. Featuring experts from around the country, the site will be an instant help site for anyone wrestling with these types of challenges.

The web possibilities are endless, and the only limit is imagination (and funding of course).

Within this new world, here are a few tips to maximize your website:

1) Think design. Today we live in a design driven culture. You may not be a designer yourself, but you need to begin recognizing the power of good design and how it can impact your church or ministry. Good design isn't just decoration, it's "connection." Designer Charles Eames said, "Design is a plan for action." Re-thinking the design elements of your website isn't just a "cosmetic" issue – it's a fundamental issue about something that connects with your audience on a very deep and significant basis.

Few things are powerful enough to unite an entire culture. Governments, dictators, business leaders, and global influencers of all kinds have spent centuries trying to discover how to bring together world; and time and time again, they've found that there is just one answer.

Design.

In the book, <u>The Substance of Style: How The Rise of Aesthetic Value is Remaking Commerce, Culture, and Consciousness</u>, Virginia Postral makes an important statement:

"Aesthetics, or styling, has become an accepted unique selling point – on a global basis. In a crowded marketplace, aesthetics is often the only way to make a product stand out."

Early in the life of the church, the Christian community discovered the transforming power of images. From Byzantine paintings and mosaics, to the great art of the middle ages and renaissance, to the icons of Eastern Orthodoxy, the church presented its message through the narrative storytelling power of images. Under Communism, Lenin exploited the influence of propaganda posters, and it didn't take long for the kings of American business to investigate the power of advertising images.

For good or bad, since the earliest days of recorded history, the power of design has influenced millions.

And now, once again, design has united a generation.

From the intense graphic design of videogames, to the pioneering special effects of major motion pictures, to the storyboards of music videos and commercials and high definition television, young people today speak the language of design.

My daughters could retouch digital photos while still in elementary school, and by middle school were accomplished web designers.

Today, we live in a design driven generation, and if the Church is going to make an impact, design is the language we must learn.

In Western culture, content has always been king. From the earliest days of the Hebrew scripture, to the spread of Christianity across Western Europe and eventually America, we've been a "word-based" people. William Tyndale's translation of the Bible into English sparked a revolution of literacy in the 16th century, and the greatest missionary efforts of the last few centuries have been the goals of translating and distributing the Biblical text to every culture and people on the planet.

As a result – and rightly so – content has been far more important than form in our art, writing, media, music, and architecture.

But today, we live in a design culture, and form has become critical to connecting with the public. So while Biblical literacy can never be taken for granted, we now face a new challenge: presenting a message of hope to a generation that's more visually sophisticated than any generation in history.

It's not hard to see, because the evidence is everywhere. Just check out the unique design features of new computers or the interior design of trendy coffee shops. Cell phones, automobiles, software, movies – all are examples of a design driven culture.

Sure, 16th Century Pope Julius could have painted the Vatican's Sistine Chapel a nice solid color, but he chose to give Michelangelo a creative challenge. We Christians should have learned from that, but today we build churches in metal buildings, design boring websites, and create tacky book and tape covers. As a producer and media consultant, I have spent decades encouraging clients to realize the power of design for connecting with customers, and recognizing its influence in getting a message heard. I recommend they reconsider worship graphics and images, product packaging, television programming, websites, publications – anything they create with a new attitude toward design. Re-thinking the design elements of a project isn't just a "cosmetic" issue – it's a fundamental issue about something that connects with the audience or customer on a very deep and significant basis.

2) Think Short – Your website biography isn't the place for a five page resume. A one or two paragraph biography is much more likely to be read. The same is true when describing your programs, outreaches, and other aspects of your church or ministry.

People READ books. They SCAN websites.

Certainly you can provide more length if the surfer wants to go deep on a particular subject. But give them the option of brevity, and they'll be more likely to come back.

3) Think Interactive – Help the web surfer connect with your ministry. The deeper they go into your site, the longer they tend to stay. Think of all the questions a visitor or new member might have and provide the answers. Create an interactive Bible study. Offer ministry resources, including sermon notes, outlines, and other information. How about behind the scenes insights from a pastor's blog? Give people a reason to come back.

4) Think Commerce – It's one thing for people to hear you for an hour on Sunday. It's something else entirely when they get your books and tapes into their home and spend more and more time in the Word. Create an online bookstore and provide teaching tapes, books, and other resources to your congregation or partners. Forty percent of product orders from television infomercials come through the Internet. People love to buy online, so make that another "connection point" to your ministry.

This isn't from hard research, but one thing I've noticed is that the longer a surfer is on your site, the less likely he or she is to buy. It appears they get distracted by interesting information and eventually forget why they came. Remember that most Internet customers are impulse buyers, so grease the skids to allow them easy access. Remind them why they came in the first place – especially if you're selling a product or requesting a donation.

5) Think Technology – Everyday the world is shrinking because of technology and our ability to outsource. When you call an airline these days looking for lost bags, it's likely someone in India will track down the bags. Another airline's reservation agents are all housewives working from their home computers in the Midwest. At the drive-thru for some fast food restaurants, your order will be to someone at a call center thousands of miles away. Your order (and your digital photo) will be relayed back to a restaurant employee standing 10-feet from you. In a world where the Internet has changed everything, you should explore how technology can enhance your website.

Pastor Greg Laurie at Harvest Church in Riverside, California uses online counselors at his Harvest Crusades for those watching the event live worldwide via the Internet. A growing number of ministries have links on their website so you can access them through cell phones. The world keeps changing, and we need to change with it.

6) Think globally: With an online presence, your church or ministry suddenly becomes a global outreach. I've received e-mails from Russia, Lithuania, Nigeria, Chile, and many more countries from people who have seen my website and responded. One church in a former Soviet republic actually began producing a Christian television program after downloading a series of TV production articles from my company's website. In that former Communist country, the people had no access to training or textbooks, and after scanning the web, discovered the library of free articles on our site. Today, they're producing a weekly Christian television program on the government TV channel using that information.

After I was interviewed on MSNBC recently, the *Manila Daily Standard* newspaper in the Philippines published an article from my website as part of its debate about banning certain movies in its country.

With the Internet, you have a remarkable opportunity to reach those who would never darken the door of your church, so don't forget to provide materials on salvation, Christian living, marriage and family, and other topics.

In the 21st Century, an Internet presence could become the most effective tool for evangelism, education, and promotion ever known. But we'll never see its potential unless we're looking toward the future.

Chapter 6

Knowing Your Audience

—ₘ—

A few years ago, a national media magazine interviewed me about the importance of audience research. Looking back at that interview might give you some insight into just how important it is to know as much as possible about your audience.

Question: As a producer, what do you find yourself wanting or needing, that audience research can provide?

Everything! That may sound a little crazy, but the fact is, television is driven by the size of its audience. You can make a living publishing books for a small readership, or having a niche magazine, or having a small church, but television is so terribly expensive, it needs to reach the widest possible audience. Therefore, I want to know anything I can that will keep the audience watching.

And it goes beyond the traditional male/female and age demographic breakdowns. I'd like to know if my audience is blue-collar or professional, educated or uneducated, religious or non-religious, etc. All these factors can help focus a program that will be more effective and compelling to that audience.

Question: How can a creative producer (or other creative leader) use research?

I use research from the very beginning of a project. For instance, at the start it helps with the decision of which project to do, and how to approach that project. Are patriotic themes "hot" right now? Are religious themes in demand? Do people want episodic dramas with continuing characters that they can follow from week to week? Is the audience interested in music or drama or documentaries?

It starts with research. As an example, in Hollywood right now, we have a term called "Post-Passion Hollywood." It's the recognition that Mel Gibson's film "The Passion of the Christ" really hit a nerve with the religious audience, and that particular audience is huge. As a result, we call the incredible box-office that came from that film "Passion Dollars." Finally, the men and women at the executive levels in Hollywood realized there was a Christian audience out there and it was substantial, and good for the bottom line. As a result, we saw the production of films like "The Lord of the Rings," "Chronicles of Narnia," "The Exorcism of Emily Rose," "Amazing Grace: The William Wilberforce Story" and others. Twentieth Century Fox has even opened a new faith oriented film distribution company.

So in that case, you can see how understanding the audience made a dramatic difference in the direction of Hollywood. How much more then, should we as Christians want to make that type of connection with our audience?

Next, we use that information to design our approach and write the script. It doesn't matter if it's a preaching program, a music program, or a dramatic program. Accurate audience information can be used to help shape and structure an interesting program.

The fact is, I wish pastors, evangelists, and Bible teachers would use research more. That doesn't mean I think they should "pander" and preach a watered-down message for "itching ears." Not at all! It simply means they should attempt to understand the struggles and frustrations of the audience, learning their hopes and dreams, so a more-effective message can be designed based on that knowledge.

I'm always amazed at how well Jesus knew His audience. The Bible says those who heard His words noted what "authority" He had. That means they found Him to be "in touch," informed, relevant, and so solid in his reasoning that none could reasonably argue. His knowledge of the audience and their times highlighted the eternal truth behind His every presentation.

Question: Doesn't research limit a producer's creativity? You know that old struggle between the creative types and the number crunchers?

That depends to a great extent on the creativity and self-confidence of the producer. Yes, there are instances where the research results are either fuzzy or indicate an approach that clashes artistically with the director's or producer's vision. In *those* cases, you should rely on the experience and track record of the producer, and go with his or her vision.

In my own case, I think people hire me as much for my track record as anything else. After three decades I've seen about everything in Christian television, and if we don't have accurate information about a particular situation, I've usually encountered it before, and know how to deal with it.

On the other hand, research is actually quite liberating. To know the audience's likes and dislikes gives you an immediate jump on the project. And it gets us past that period of wondering which way to go, or how to approach the subject. But I have to admit – it usually takes some seasoning for a producer not to be intimidated by the data and to use it effectively.

The best place to see research working side by side with directors and producers is in commercials. The commercials you see on television are usually supported by a mountain of research – but the spots are typically still highly creative and entertaining.

Question: Why doesn't Christian broadcasting do more research?

Two reasons: First of all, most Christian television stations and ministries are on very tight budgets. And unfortunately, the research budget is often the first thing tossed out the window. It's sad really, because research is often the key to discovering what mistakes are being made, and in what direction a television program should be headed. In other words, the very thing that could save you is what's being discarded.

But that's because of reason number two: Inexperience. Once again, many ministries and television stations are also very short sighted. Historically, they want an answer *now* – they can't wait for data to be tabulated, and they aren't interested in what will work 5 to ten years from now. Yet that attitude results in always being behind. How often have you heard jokes about how Christian television is always about ten years behind secular television in style, look, and professionalism? That's a key reason.

Once of my strongest desires is to create a funding organization devoted to discovering what we should be producing 5 to ten years from today. I would like to find the finances to bring in talented researchers, writers, producers, directors, and other creative people, to explore the future of media and how Christians can continue to make an impact.

Until we begin doing that, we'll always be behind the curve.

Question: But if Christian broadcasters are prayerfully following God's will, why should they need research?

I'm really tired of this one. Let's finally put it to rest. If this principle were true, we wouldn't need to have police to protect us, alarms to wake us, and doctors to fix us when we're sick. And we certainly wouldn't need to raise money for Christian television – God would take care of all of it.

But we live in a horribly broken and fallen world. Occasionally, God intervenes in our affairs and performs wonderful miracles – but because He is sovereign, we don't always know when or where He will act. Therefore, we need to use the brains, insight, and knowledge He's given us to fulfill our mission on the earth.

Essentially, what we're doing is *evangelism* – finding the most effective way to preach the gospel message to as many people as possible. If understanding how my audience thinks, reacts, and responds increases my chances of getting through to them, then I'm going to take advantage of that kind of research. To not do that is to turn our backs on marvelous information and tools that God has given us.

Question: Can we become slaves to research?

Absolutely. I've worked recently with an organization that is paralyzed by the perceived need for more research on everything. They are literally terrified of acting, and as a result, spend thousands of dollars on focus groups, questionnaires, interviews, and other research. On the surface, *they want to be absolutely sure.* But in reality, it isn't because the information will actually help them, it's because they are terrified of change. That's why some pastors or ministry leaders delay acting with the response, "If I just had one more report, or one more piece of information, I would make a decision."

I was at a Los Angeles Angel's baseball game in Anaheim not long ago with leadership expert John Maxwell, and told him about my frustrations with a client. His reply was that when a leader has at least 65 percent of the information he or she needs, it's time to make a decision.

Maxwell knows that information and research are helpful, but we can't let it paralyze our decision making.

Christian Media At the Dawn of
The New Millennium

—〰—

I've always been fascinated with the remarkable story of missionary-adventurer David Livingstone and his search for the source of the Nile River. During his last journey, and after years without contact with the outside world, the parallel story of journalist Henry Morton Stanley's search for Livingstone is one of the legendary rescue stories of all time. Livingstone had been to Africa many times and was considered one of the greatest British explorers in history. I've been told that when he sent a message to his supporters to send more men to Africa to assist in his missionary work, they responded: "Send us maps so we will know which roads to take to get there." Livingstone answered: "Don't send men who will come only if there are roads. I want men who will go where there are no roads."

I often remember that story when I think about the future of Christian media, and the men and women we'll need to pioneer it's uncharted territory. As we're just off the starting line of the next thousand-year cycle of our history, for many people it's a time of fear, anticipation, and trepidation. For others, it's a time of excitement and anticipation. But for those of us who spend our lives working in the media, it should be a time of deep reflection and evaluation.

Are we utilizing the most effective media techniques and strategies for the gospel? Are we making a dent in the culture war? Are we making a difference in people's lives? Is the money we spend worth it?

These are the questions that keep me awake at night. So often, we spend our time wondering about lighting equipment, the newest non-linear editing system, a new film stock, high definition technology, or an innovative audio board, when the essential question should be *is this working? Are people being reached and changed because of what we're doing?*

Especially at this remarkable time in history, I've been thinking a great deal about how our task will continue to change in the next century. How will entering the "digital age" effect Christian media? And what changes will occur in the immediate future that will impact our mission to reach the world with the good news of Jesus Christ?

I'm no expert on technology – in fact, I've given that up long ago. I realized that if I tried to keep up with computer and technological innovation, I would have time for little else. And that's when I discovered that it isn't the technology that's important – it's the way we use it that will ultimately make the difference.

I'm reminded of the Internet and the recent explosion of *data*. Everyday, someone is developing a remarkable new way to move, manipulate, or update *information*. But *moving information* and *gaining wisdom and insight* are two entirely different things. In your own work, are you simply "moving information around?" Or are you gaining wisdom and insight?

Don't focus on the technology – focus on how that technology is used.

The Internet itself won't save or transform anyone's life. But how we use the Internet and what we put on it, might.

And that's why I have created some key areas that will be critical for accomplishing this goal, especially as we begin the next century. These are areas I believe will always be important regardless of changes in technology, culture, and trends.

America's greatest playwright, Eugene O'Neill, concentrated his work on the "eternal verities" – *the things that last*. He wasn't concerned about trends, or the latest article in popular magazines or entertainment programs. He was concerned about the eternal questions that we wrestle with from generation to generation.

Similarly, in the world of Christian media there are "eternal verities" – *areas that are critical to remind us that what we're doing matters.* Areas that will never change, no matter if it's a digital or analog camera we're shooting with, or what type of microphone we use, or what type of lighting instrument we plug in. These eternal verities include:

1) Our ability to tell a story. Once again, it's critically important to remember that ultimately we're telling a story. It's a simple story about how God chose to become one of us and share His eternal plan with people who didn't deserve it. It's not about close-ups, cuts and dissolves, better limiters, or higher video resolution. It's about telling a story. That's why as we enter the digital age of the next century, let's spend more time learning how to tell a story more effectively. I don't worry about when we'll change our Christian TV stations to the new high-resolution format as much as when we'll start producing dramatic movies and television programs that *tell a story.* It doesn't matter the program format – *preaching, music, documentary, variety, whatever,* the program should tell some type of story. Until that story is told most effectively, the audience is not going to be interested.

Why are Christian media producers not producing more dramatic projects? That's another book. But part of the problem is our inability to tell a story. Stories touch people, and change their lives.

Let's make a new commitment to storytelling, and understand that unless we can tell a powerful story, our chances of reaching our audience are terribly diminished.

2) Forget Christian "lingo." A few years ago, I listened to a remarkable story on National Public Radio that focused on a major citywide evangelistic effort by one of our largest churches in the West. First of all, I was amazed that NPR would even do a feature on this type of Christian story. Second, I was completely prepared for the secular reporter to make a mockery of the event, and trivialize Christian faith as so many have done in the past. But quite the contrary, the report was genuinely open-minded, and attempted to tell a balanced, sincere story. The reporter even questioned her own need for a personal faith, and openly wondered if this might be her moment for an encounter with God.

What I *wasn't* prepared for was her difficulty in getting Christians to describe their faith in *normal human language*. Time after time, when she would interview the church members, they used terminology that only a Christian would understand. *Faith walk, strongholds of the enemy, salvation, praying through, born again, dominions, reaching the lost* – all these are terms for which a non-Christian has little or no understanding.

Here was an incredible chance on *National* Public Radio to explain the life-changing experience of Christ's love to a nation-wide audience, and yet the reporter could not find a single person in that church who could explain their experience in simple terms anyone could understand. Finally, the reporter walked away frustrated, deciding that since it was so difficult to explain, it must not be relevant to our culture or to her personally.

I was devastated. When I read the New Testament, Jesus doesn't use a single word of Christian "lingo." He doesn't use theological or philosophical terms. And he certainly doesn't talk over people's heads.

Jesus understood that the way to reach people was to speak to them in everyday language. Why have we lost that ability? Why have we created an entire vocabulary of words and phrases that only church members comprehend?

One of my closest friends is a college buddy who today is a respected and successful physician. I've noticed when he's talking to his staff or conferring with other doctors in the hospital, he uses a vocabulary particular to his profession – words and phrases that are very specific and effective, but for which I have little or no understanding. However, when he talks to his patients, he speaks in a style *they* understand – explaining difficult medical concepts in a simple, yet effective way. His language is effective enough to give his patients an accurate understanding of their medical condition.

Why can't we do that as Christians? In a church, college, Bible school class or teaching session, it's fine to use sophisticated words and phrases that more accurately describe the spiritual and theological concepts we're discussing. But, we have to be more sensitive when we're dealing with non-Christians, speaking in a language and style they understand.

Let's make a renewed commitment to express our faith through sermons, television, radio, motion pictures, and other media in a style and language that reaches everyday people from all walks of life. If Jesus did it, then we can do it too.

3. Staying current. While it's important that we tell effective stories and use language and phrases people understand, it's also critical that we put these media efforts in packages that people want to open. If you have a Christian television channel in your home, then turn the sound off and switch between that channel and ABC, MTV, MSNBC, or the Sci-Fi Channel. In most cases, you'll notice a difference.

Look at the video quality, the graphic presentation, the shooting style of secular networks. These channels are designed to capture an audience. Jesus dealt with current issues, and he did it in the surroundings that were popular – *the marketplace, the homes of the rich and powerful, the temple square* – all places where he knew people would listen to His message. We need to package our message in an innovative and exciting way so people will want to watch and listen.

I saw a magazine ad recently for a Christian college, and the tag line was: *"We're not ashamed of the old-fashioned gospel."* Of course, I've heard that over-used line before. But this time I thought: *What* is *the "old-fashioned gospel"?* The gospel message of the 1950s? The gospel message of the 1800s? American needs the gospel message that *Jesus* preached – the same one that's true *today!* A message that has an answer for the hopelessness of the inner city, a message that has an answer for the school violence that's swallowing up our young people, and a message that has an answer for those caught in a web of pornography and drugs.

Non-believers aren't looking for an "old-fashioned" answer. They're looking for *today's* answer, and unless we can produce programs and events that portray our message as an answer for *today,* they'll never listen.

Let's make a renewed commitment to use current techniques and styles in an effort to more effectively reach an audience that desperately needs it.

4) New financing models: I had a discussion with a Christian television station owner recently who was absolutely convinced that God had ordained telethons in order to finance Christian television. He was totally confident that no other way was acceptable to God but telethons, and we had no business using other methods of financing Christian television.

If telethons are working for your church, station, or ministry, then by all means continue. But the fact is, as we enter the new millennium, we're also going to need alternative ways to finance Christian media, or we'll continue to lag behind in our task. Currently in television the preferred method is to offer a product on the air to capture "names." Then, those names are contacted over and over again through fundraising efforts in the mail.

There's really nothing wrong with that approach *(unless the fundraising appeals are offensive, unethical or in poor taste)*; however, that approach has done little to raise the massive funding necessary to make Christian movies, dramatic TV series, and other types of expensive programming.

But why is that necessary? Why do we need these types of programs?

Because they work. They capture audiences by the millions. Remember storytelling?

Believe me, if preaching and teaching on television generated great audiences, the secular networks would be producing those types of programs in prime time. But what are they doing? They produce *TV movies, sitcoms, and dramatic series programming.*

I don't have all the answers for this dilemma, but I want to continue raising the question. When we can change the financing model for Christian broadcasting, moviemaking, and producing, we will literally change the face of Christian media.

Wouldn't it be nice not to have to struggle with equipment that's falling apart? Wouldn't it be nice to be able to travel to far away locations for special programs? Wouldn't it be nice to be able to work with professional writers, producers, directors, and actors to accomplish your goals?

Financing is the key. When we change the financing model, we'll change history.

Let's make a renewed commitment to explore other financing options – sponsorship, grants, commercial breaks, etc. – in order to open up our programs to better and more effective funding.

5) A new vision for media: At Cooke Pictures, the production and consulting company my wife and I founded, we've made a decision to re-evaluate our vision for producing Christian media programming. Upon reflection, we saw that we were being asked to work with a number of clients who really didn't have much of a vision for television, and therefore weren't very interested in being innovative and cutting edge. It wasn't necessarily a budget issue, although in media finances are always an issue at some level.

Mostly, it was a *commitment* issue.

Who knows why some clients want to produce television programs? Perhaps it's ego, popularity, pressure from family, friends or church members – it could be most anything.

But this year, we've decided to really focus on clients who had a genuine calling and commitment to change lives through media and were willing to do whatever it takes creatively to make that happen.

Another Christian producer recently said: "The world is full of media companies that are out to make a buck. The world desperately needs a media company that is out to make a difference."

We want to be a media company that makes a difference, and I would urge you to reevaluate your own vision for the media. If you work with a station manager, pastor or other ministry leader, I suggest you sit down with him or her and discuss their vision as well. Ask the hard questions, and don't settle for easy answers.

The cost is great, and the stakes are high.

At the beginning of a new millennium, we can't afford to have churches, ministries, stations, or production companies wasting time and money. We need people, companies, and organizations that are committed – *not* to technology, but to *using* that technology to reach people with a message than can change their lives.

Appendix

Appendix I

Producing a Christmas Pageant Or Other Special Event

—⟋m⟍—

Every winter, church media producers across the country prepare for a time-honored and terrifying ritual: "The Church Christmas Pageant."

These local church sponsored theatrical presentations are usually videotaped for archives or bookstore sales, and although everyone begins the process with high hopes, the ultimate events often leave media producers sobbing, or mumbling that they will "never do it again!"

NOTE: If you're such a producer, and you're reading this later than July, you should have already started working on this year's Christmas presentation. Whether you have or not, and in hopes of helping you keep both your sanity and family intact, here are some tips from the Cooke Pictures archives to help make this Christmas season a little more joyful:

1) It's never too early to start preparing. Year after year, producers wait until the last minute, thinking: I'll let the Music Director do all of his work first. Nothing could be worse. Start planning now. Get your hands on a script and music as early as possible, and start thinking immediately about staging and shooting. Certainly things will change, but experienced producers and directors know it's easier to change an existing plan than to create one from scratch at the last minute.

2) Bring your crew into the process as early as is feasible. Start generating excitement and ideas from your volunteers and crew-members. They usually want to offer suggestions and ideas, but are rarely asked. Remember: You don't have to use all their ideas. But giving them a good listen will motivate them to be more-committed members of the team and generally perpetuate better morale.

3) Help the music director understand the differences between "stage lighting" and "television lighting." What's the point of going to the trouble and expense of shooting the Christmas musical if your end product's video level won't register? Help the pageant's music director understand the limitations of the camera. Don't be obnoxious or know-it-all; just work with him or her and help them understand. Also, be sensitive to the music director's spirit and vision. Supplement the lighting where necessary, but do your best not to "blast" the stage and ruin the dramatic experience.

4) Create a shot list. Most church TV directors try to "wing it" and hope they can stay on top of things during the performance. Don't take chances. Create a shot list during the rehearsals. That way, when you get to the actual performances you can relax a little and concentrate on the timing of your cuts and dissolves. Certainly there will be changes and adjustments, but that's minor compared to all the screaming and yelling you'll have to do if you're not prepared. And speaking of that:

5) Stop screaming and yelling. A screaming director is a director who's out of ideas. Every member of your team loses a little respect for you as soon as you start yelling. Learn to control your temper, and guide your crew through the program with encourage-ment, strong leadership skills, and creative ideas and suggestions. I've often advised young directors to read Dale Carnegie's classic book, How to Win Friends and Influence People. It's the best book I've found on this subject, filled with insights and techniques for how to achieve your goals through other people.

6) Know the difference between "cuts" and "dissolves." Cuts and dissolves to a television director are like periods and commas to a writer. They are the visual grammar that makes the scene work.

They express two completely different feelings and emotions, so don't mix them up. Remember: Cuts are sharp and make the scene move. Dissolves are softer, slower, and on the "warm and fuzzy" side. Understand how to use each technique effectively, and your programs will instantly take a giant leap forward.

7) Shoot at least one rehearsal specifically for the video presentation. During the actual performance, you can't get the camera onstage for the unique close-ups and angles you really need. So I always suggest you shoot a dress rehearsal. That will allow you to put a camera onstage, backstage, or within a group of actors to get a unique angle or perspective. Don't overdo it, but it's a great way to find powerful shots that you can intercut into your final edit.

8) Have a debriefing. Don't dare release the crew without a short meeting on what worked and what didn't during the night's taping. You can learn a great deal by discussing the shoot with the crew, and find out helpful information for the next night. It's not a time for flogging the crew – it's a time for evaluation, motivation, and encouragement.

9) Toss out the normal rules for shooting a church service. A Christmas program is completely different from a Sunday service, so why aren't you changing your camera positions? Set the appropriate camera angles for each project you shoot, and never leave them in the same place for everything. Those cameras are the gateway for thousands of people to understand your presentation, so use them effectively and in the right places.

Remember: The Christmas season is supposed to be a time of joy, not tears. So start thinking now about a successful and effective way to tape this year's Christmas play or musical presentation. Some churches spend hundreds of thousands of dollars on their shows, and it's the one time of the year when you'll be most likely to get significant numbers of non-Christians into the building.

Give them something to remember during the program, and also give them something on video to take home and enjoy for years to come.

Appendix II

Videotaping Religious Conferences

—ɷ—

K nowing I had produced and directed literally hundreds of church and ministry conferences and events around the world, Barry Cobus, founder and editor of "Technologies for Worship" magazine asked if we could talk about the pros and cons of video-taping religious conferences.

Barry Cobus: What are some of the most important reasons for videotaping religious conferences?

Phil Cooke: There are actually a number of significant reasons to videotape religious conferences and conventions. Since most of these conferences involve teaching and preaching, first, you can offer the conference on CD or DVD to your attendees, members, or supporters as teaching tools. Many times, it's important for people to have a permanent copy to review later for learning purposes, archival purposes, or strictly as a way to remember the event. In fact, when I shoot a conference, I often have a company come in who can actually copy the videotapes or DVD's on high-speed recorders and have the products available to sell right there at the conference.

Think of how the impact of your conference can be extended when the attendees have a copy to take home and show their friends, family, and business associates. Needless to say, this is not only a great service to the participants, but selling the CD/DVD material can also positively impact the financial bottom line.

Also, it often makes great material for a religious television program. You can see many ministries on television right now who use their conferences and meetings as the primary source of material for their television outreach. Why? Because at conferences, people come with real excitement and expectancy, and when that's captured on video it often makes wonderful television.

Video can be used to tie two separate locations together, or introduce a guest from another location. A relatively recent example of this is the Promise Keepers events, where they have conducted two gatherings simultaneously in different cities, linking them with video transmitted via satellite. Each meeting can "talk to" and "see" each other through the video transmission.

One church conference in the Midwest distributed satellite downlink dishes to about 200 churches throughout the United States. While the main conference was happening at one location, thousands of people who couldn't attend could come to their local church and watch the event "live" as it happened and join in the service. Using technology like that, the conference went in size from the normal 8,000 at the actual event, to more than 50,000 connected via satellite. Now, with live video streaming, the same can be done through the Internet. I'm very excited about the possibilities technology like this opens to religious conferences, concerts, and other events.

So you can see that from low-budget situations to high budget situations, videotaping can really enhance the effectiveness and impact of a religious conference.

BC: So even if I have a small budget, videotaping my conference can make a difference?

PC: Absolutely. For one thing, you are building an important archive for the future. Having all the speakers, music, and special events at your conference recorded allows you to have a permanent archive for later reference. Plus, by selling the tapes or discs of the conference either to the attendees, or later, to your members and supporters gives you another avenue for marketing and fundraising.

BC: So where do I start?

PC: First of all, I strongly urge that those who are holding a conference find a producer with experience in shooting conferences and conventions. There are many differences between shooting in arenas versus shooting in a studio or church, and you need to find someone with experience in both. I would suggest you look for a ministry or religious organization you respect and admire who has recorded conferences. Call them and ask their media director or television producer. They should be happy to give you ideas and advice, or the names of qualified producers.

BC: What about equipment?

PC: When you find the right producer, he or she will be able to advise you on the right cameras and equipment for the job. Sometimes, the arena will have camera equipment for rent, and other times, you'll have to bring it in from the outside. Either way, your producer will be able to guide you to the right decision based on your budget.

BC: Is there a difference between shooting the conference for video and shooting for television?

PC: If you think you might want to use the footage on a television program, commercial, or broadcast promotional campaign, then you should definitely use higher quality camera equipment and record on a higher level. For those unfamiliar with broadcast standards, as I write this, the normal videotape format with most Christian producers for shooting broadcast television programming is called BetaSP. However, the new DV, Mini-DV, and DVC Pro formats are all digital formats that have remarkable picture quality and would definitely qualify for broadcast. We're also in the middle of the transition to High Definition video, and while that will become the standard for the future, it will also involve many different videotape and disk formats. Again, an experienced producer can help you navigate through those waters.

If broadcast television isn't in your future plans, then less expensive camera equipment and formats are available. Certainly, there are some instances where these formats are also used on television, but by and large, their uses are mostly confined to industrial, corporate, training, and other non-broadcast venues.

BC: What are the most common mistakes religious organizations make in the production of videos produced from conventions?

PC: Understanding just how unique and different the medium of television really is. I've said before in this book that a light bulb is not a candle you plug into a wall. A car is not a horse with wheels. A television is not a radio with pictures. A successful video program is not just a videotaped religious service or conference.

Television and video have their own strengths and weaknesses, and those strengths and weaknesses need to be properly exploited if we are to be as effective as we possibly can with that medium.

A videotaped religious service is not the most effective use of the medium, but today, church and religious services probably represent the vast majority of religious video programming. That's not to say that sermons, teaching situations, conferences and conventions shouldn't be on television, but they need to be done in a more innovative way that takes advantage of the medium.

For instance, in a live convention or conference you're sitting in a crowd of (we hope) interested people. You experience firsthand the worship and music, you can feel the electricity of the moment, and you can often sense the energy and the excitement as the speaker paces back and forth across the stage.

But when you watch that convention on video or television, you're often by yourself, watching the service through a glass TV screen from the other side of the room – and more than likely, you're also doing something else at the time – cooking, reading, or getting dressed. Very few of the things that make it exciting in a live situation come through as you watch it later on television.

Therefore, we need to take advantage of creative video and television techniques to translate that event into as powerful a program as possible. The most successful producers today are the ones who are well versed in those techniques and know how to transform a live event into a compelling television experience.

BC: In your lectures and workshops, you often speak on the topic "Increasing Your Effectiveness On-Camera." When you work with pastors, evangelists, teachers, religious leaders, program hosts, actors, and other on-camera personalities, what are some of the secrets to effectiveness?

PC: Don't get locked into one style of preaching or teaching on camera. For instance, just because you're a pastor or teacher doesn't mean that you have to do everything standing behind a podium. One of my greatest joys is taking pastors who think they can only function well behind a podium, into other settings – a living room, a back alley, a beach, a homeless shelter, a desert, a mission field, etc. They're quite often thrilled and amazed to discover the possibilities of ministering in more creative and unconventional settings.

Also, talk to one person. Whether you're preaching, teaching, or hosting a conference or convention and you're being recorded, don't think about those millions of people in TV land – think about one person. There's no way you can effectively focus on ministry while trying to imagine the multitude of needs, hurts, questions, and struggles of the entire television or video audience. So calm down and focus on one person, just as if you were talking to a friend. You'll be amazed at the difference it will make.

Know your audience. Beyond the immediate audience at the conference or convention, learn about audience demographics and talk to your producer about who is in your audience. Until you discover who's watching out there, how can you be most effective?

Aside from producing and directing media projects, I have always had a heart for helping local church and ministry organizations improve the quality of their video and television programs. The fact is, every program produced within the religious community reflects on us all, and therefore each of us needs to be doing everything we can to improve Christian programming.

I've discovered that most organizations are concerned about the real, practical, day-to-day aspects of producing video and television programs: Should I shoot my conference or religious service? Should I rent or purchase equipment? What type of equipment should I use? Where will I find a crew? What about music? How about fundraising? Where can I find a director?

I believe that most people are already convinced that video, television and motion pictures are important avenues of extending their Christian faith – they just need practical information on how and where to start. Looking around, I couldn't find a single book that answered those questions, so I decided to write one – <u>Successful Christian Television</u>. It was my first book, and it was written for anyone who's ever watched current religious television and thought: "I can do better than that, but I don't know where to start." The book represents decades of producing religious programs, and the information would easily cost hundreds of thousands of dollars if you hired a consultant. But now it's all in one reference book, available in bookstores nationwide.

BC: So what's next for Phil Cooke?

PC: First of all, I'm actually very excited about recording religious conferences and conventions. As I said before, technology is opening up some fascinating doors that we only dreamed about a few years ago. We have to keep moving forward and my great challenge in life is moving out there into unexplored territory. Even with its risks and dangers, it's an exciting place to be, and it's the only place a real breakthrough in Christian broadcasting will happen.

Second, one of my great passions has always been to produce and direct motion pictures. That's always been a difficulty for religious organizations because of the high expense and lack of quality of many past projects. We are currently developing projects along that line, and I think it's one of the critical places where we can have a voice and make an impact in our contemporary culture.

Third, I want to stay on top of what's happening in the Internet world. I created a website at <u>philcooke.com</u> that features my blog on issues of media, faith, and culture. It's critically important that we keep the conversation going with the culture if we're going to be heard. Our production and consulting company, Cooke Pictures, has an interesting site at <u>cookepictures.com</u> that's designed to be a resource for religious program producers and organizations. At this one site we want people to be able to download program budget worksheets, storyboard forms, information on equipment, creative techniques, leadership principles, and more.

I believe we're in a remarkable state of change in this culture, and anything that will bring us closer together for information or inspiration, I'm all for it.

Appendix III

The Secrets of Shooting Overseas

—⟋⟍—

S hooting overseas? Never leave your ingenuity at home. After producing programming in more than 30 (mostly third-world) countries around the globe, I've discovered that in tough foreign situations, it's often the most unusual ideas that work best. I've been caught up in two military coups in Africa, held up by drug lords in Ecuador, had equipment confiscated in the Middle East, and nearly killed in a fall from a helicopter shooting in the Caribbean, so there's not too much that would throw me today.

As anyone knows who has much experience in producing radio or television programming overseas, the frustrations and struggles come from an infinite number of places – places where we rarely experience trouble at home. For instance, checking in at a hotel in America is usually a breeze. But overseas, that normally simple act can be a nightmare.

Renting cars, checking in at airports, renting and clearing equipment, making a phone call – all can be a wild experience overseas, especially in what we consider "third-world" countries.

Case in point: On one of my first overseas shoots in the late 1970s, the customs officers of a large South American country held $250,000 of our production equipment for five days. They would offer no reason, except for "paperwork being processed."

I tried everything.

I was scheduled to be shooting near the headwaters of the Amazon River at great financial cost, and my patience was running thin. But all I could do was continue to show up each morning, bright and early, on the doorstep of the customs office.

Finally, on the fifth day, the managing customs officer asked if I could prove that I was really a legitimate television and motion picture director from the United States (forget that we were bringing in a quarter million dollars in television equipment).

I had to stop and think. After all, it's not like we directors carry around a "TV & Film License" or anything. But I started looking through my wallet anyway – and that's when it hit me.

I pulled out my old tattered membership card from the American Film Institute. In those days, the AFI was just beginning, and the membership card represented little more than a subscription to the foundation's monthly magazine.

But when I whipped out the card, the man was stunned and amazed.

"You're a member of the American Film Institute?!" he asked with the reverence of a religious pilgrim. He had no clue what the AFI was, but he sure thought it sounded impressive.

"Of course I am," I shot back, as if the AFI was an "official" government institute for all American filmmakers.

"Why didn't you say so!" he replied, and with much pomp and ceremony, he immediately ushered me and my crew into a warehouse where our equipment was kept – and even offered a special police escort to our hotel.

I never realized how important that simple magazine subscription would be!

Since that time, as a writer and director, I have traveled with the Bedouins in the Middle East, taken a freighter up to the headwaters of the Amazon, explored game reserves in Africa, confronted witch doctors in Haiti, and stared down the barrels of automatic weapons shortly after a coup in Nigeria. By the very nature of my work, I rarely go to the posh resorts. Worse yet, I'm often sent to countries that are often socially and economically unstable.

But it's important to point out that being prepared doesn't mean having a condescending attitude or being racist. I never recommend you bully your way through any situation – in fact, that's precisely the type of behavior that will land you in a foreign jail (and foreign jails are, shall we say, not the most pleasant places to land). The fact is, we often have the skills necessary to accomplish anything here in the United States – but in other countries, it's a different game completely.

Whether shooting in royal palaces in Austria, or carrying equipment through the Amazon jungle, there are important skills and techniques necessary to getting your project back home, both professionally and on budget.

And during those often difficult times, I discovered some important keys for making those trips (especially low budget trips) a little easier, including:

1) Never attract attention as a film or video producer. If you can possibly pass for a tourist (although perhaps a "well-equipped tourist"), do it. Never lie or do anything illegal, but don't bring undue attention to yourself as an American filmmaker or television producer. There are often very expensive bonds and other fees required when bringing in television and film equipment – not to mention people looking for tips and bribes. If you can avoid those fees, you'll save quite a bit of money. After all, in many countries, it's up to the immediate discretion of the local official whether to charge you a bond, insurance fees, entry fees, or a host of other expensive charges.

Believe me, they see American movies and television programs and often figure this is their big chance to get rich. So dump your ego and be gracious and considerate – and above all, don't flaunt your expensive equipment.

It's easier today with smaller, more compact DV (digital video) equipment, but you still have to be alert.

A number of years ago, while clearing customs in one African country, I made the mistake of unpacking all my equipment cases so the customs officer could easily see each piece of equipment. But once those cases were opened and our expensive-looking television equipment popped out, customs agents, police, and even military men swarmed around the equipment like bees looking for honey. They were deeply fascinated about how the equipment worked, how much it cost, and "Are you an American TV producer?"

Fortunately, my crew was with me and could keep an eye out to make sure nothing was stolen. On the downside, once the customs officer saw the fascination around my equipment, he decided he had to charge a high customs fee. That would help him justify to his superiors why the airport nearly shut down so all the employees could get a better look.

Needless to say, it took a great deal of negotiation to get the price down to anything reasonable. He wanted so much money I was forced to leave part of the equipment locked in customs security until I was ready to leave the country. I couldn't even afford the customs fee to bring it in.

I learned a very important lesson about remaining low-key and quiet while traveling with expensive equipment.

2) Be bold when necessary. Without doing anything rash or stupid, don't be afraid to present yourself as a confident person who knows exactly what you want. Often, local officials can be influenced or persuaded to let you go without any hassle – especially if they believe you might be important enough to get them into trouble later. But remember there's a fine line between confidence and arrogance. I find most customs officials to be normal everyday people who are more than willing to work with you – but, don't push your luck.

I've said before that I recommend you get a copy of Dale Carnegie's classic book, <u>How To Win Friends And Influence People</u>. It's one of the great books of all time on how to deal with difficult people and still accomplish your goal. In many situations it doesn't matter if you are correct or not. In these circumstances, arguing from a logical perspective does no good.

It's especially true when you're being hassled by someone who doesn't speak your language, knows nothing about television, is making a few dollars a day, and probably has a fourth-grade education.

Therefore, always be gracious and considerate, but at the same time learn the skills necessary to communicate and persuade even the most obstinate people – you'll find it will help you as much in the United States as anywhere else in the world!

3) Know someone on the inside. Whenever possible, I use a contact on the inside of the country to "pave the way" by getting signatures, approvals, and other documentation completed ahead of time. Have them meet you at the airport and walk you through the right steps – it can really make a difference. This person doesn't need to be a government or business official – although that helps. A local pastor, ministry leader, missionary, or other contact is fine. If you don't know a local person who knows the language, at least send a location or production manager in a week or two before to prepare for the crew's arrival.

I've discovered that missionaries make excellent "in-country" contacts, even though they may know little about television or film. Because of the unique nature of their work, they usually have extensive experience dealing with government officials and know the local laws and regulations very well. (Not to mention their knowledge of food, locale, and transportation). In addition, they know local hardware dealers, electrical repair shops, supply houses – all important resources in the event you need emergency equipment or supplies.

4) Never underestimate the power of corrupt local officials. Once, even after completing all the proper documents, I still had to spend almost $2,000 in bribes just to get our equipment and people out of one third world airport. After that much expense, I told my cameraman to physically go with the equipment all the way to the plane, just to make sure it was delivered.

We didn't hear from him again for three hours. After a frantic search, we discovered he had been arrested outside the plane and tossed in jail (conveniently located in the basement of the airport). After another thousand in bribes, we finally got him out and were on our way.

I learned then, sometimes you can sing and dance around local officials, and other times it's important to know when they mean business.

Those of us who have traveled extensively tend to minimize the danger involved in working in politically or economically unstable countries. But the tragic fact is, missionaries, Christian workers, and journalists are being killed each year in a wide variety of countries. Therefore I can't over emphasize even on the most mundane trips, learn the location and phone number of the American Embassy, the American Express office, or stable banks and other institutions including hospitals and police stations.

5) Whenever possible, use an experienced and qualified crew. I especially recommend finding a location/production manager who is familiar with these situations. Even on low budget shoots, I can't emphasize that enough. The production crew is too busy worrying about the creative and technical aspects of the shoot. Someone else needs to worry about transportation, visas, passports, shipping documents, insurance, permits, and the multitude of other aspects of foreign production.

If you don't know of a person, contact another production company or ministry who has had that experience and get recommendations from them. In our case, we have developed relationships with people in places like Africa, Israel, Europe, Asia, and South America. They speak the language and often know the intricacies of television production as well.

I also believe in the importance of engineers. Before the age of digital technology, I once had an appointment in Africa to interview the Royal Family of Swaziland on camera, but the intense humidity caused the video tape machine to jam the night before. I would have been completely lost, but our engineer stayed up all night, pulling the equipment apart piece by piece until he corrected the problem.

The interview went flawlessly.

During the bomb scares of the mid-seventies, I was sent to Israel to cover a mission effort among the Bedouin tribes of the desert. At that time, equipment wasn't nearly as portable as today, so we shipped our cameras, video equipment and lights in a large wooden crate. When we arrived in the country we discovered the Israeli security team in New York had not only opened the crate, but dissected each piece of equipment circuit board by circuit board looking for explosives. Of course, when they finished, not knowing how to re-assemble the equipment, they just tossed the boards, gears, and belts back into the crate, nailed it shut and sent it on.

Standing in the airport warehouse in Tel Aviv, we opened the crate in horror.

But after our initial shock we carried the equipment to our hotel, and once again, thanks to the engineers on the shoot, we were able to slowly re-assemble each piece of equipment and the shoot went as planned.

Don't scrimp on talent.

6) Finally, don't get discouraged. Remember, there will be plenty of struggles with difficult communication, corrupt officials, confusing information, different rules, and frustrating local customs. But the countries that are often the most difficult, also have the most on-screen magic. You just can't duplicate here in the states what can be captured in many of these potentially volatile situations. Also, especially in ministry broadcasting, the most effective ministries are usually working in the most difficult places. But the chance to report on what God is doing in these often forgotten and out of the way places is remarkable and unforgettable.

Therefore, stay with it – you'll be very glad you did. Besides, the experiences make great stories to tell your kids!

While shooting a mission outreach to a large Bedouin tribe in the deserts of Israel we encountered a Bedouin leader who invited us to his tent for a meal. Along with a delightful collection of unusual foods, we were also offered a hearty drink of rancid, chunky goat's milk that had been "curing" inside the carcass of a dead goat in the heat of the desert sun for nearly two weeks.

The crew and I looked at each other in disbelief. We knew it would be the height of rudeness to turn down their "gracious" offer, and seeing an array of ancient Bedouin swords standing in the corner, we realized we had little choice. Then, our video engineer hit upon an idea that might distract the royal family. He had learned a technique years ago in the service where he could punch a tiny hole in the end of an egg and literally "blow" the entire egg through the hole, leaving the shell completely intact.

Desperate to try anything to keep from drinking the milk, we gave it a shot.

It worked!

The Bedouin leader was so delighted he asked the engineer to do it again and again. After four or five eggs, it began to get dark outside the tent, and before long, it was time for us to leave. Graciously, we thanked the royal family for their hospitality and quickly left the tent without having to drink the dreaded sour milk.

I've never forgotten that incident and have always been grateful for the ingenuity of our video engineer. I've never made fun of the odd or peculiar talents of my crew members since.

Successful shooting overseas begins with solid planning. During the early stages of planning a shoot overseas, there are a number of places to start:

1) Check the tourist resources. Start by checking a guidebook for the country at the local bookstore travel section. There are excellent travel guidebooks available from a variety of perspectives and publishers. These guidebooks have come a long way in the last few years and often have information relating to visas, travel advisories, medical concerns, current political situations, currency, key addresses and phone numbers, and other critical information.

2) Talk to your local travel agent. If they haven't been to the country lately it's likely they will know someone who has. That referral can provide you with first hand information about practical aspects of the trip such as airport check-in, taxis, hotels, etc.

3) Check entertainment industry resources. More and more countries are trying to attract Hollywood to shoot movies and television programs in their country because of the positive economic impact. In response, an entire industry has grown up around location shooting. Important information can be found in industry directories such as the "Blu-Book Directory" or "LA411". Internet sites like www.movie-locations.com can help as well. The best sources can be the film production office in each country, which is hosted by a local film commission.

Film Commissions

Extremely informative and helpful sources for location shooting are local and international Film Commissions. Because of the financial boon location shooting often brings to the local economy, these commissions are set-up by the local government expressly to attract television and film producers to their countries.

Most Christian producers have yet to use this wonderful resource, but I would encourage you to contact the appropriate commission on your next project. Their sole purpose is to make your experience easy and enjoyable, and they don't charge a penny for their help and assistance.

That assistance includes:

Finding local crews and equipment.

Making hotel and travel arrangements.

Cutting through red tape and regulations.

Finding scenic and historic locations to film.

And don't think you have to be a major motion picture to use their services. They are very helpful no matter what size crew. Plus, you'll find Film Commissions not only in highly industrialized countries, but also in places as diverse as Thailand, Guatemala, Chile, Malta, Jamaica, Israel, and Poland. Plus, there's an office in all 50 American states.

Appendix IV

A Special Word about Shooting in Israel:

—〜〜—

S ooner or later most ministries have the desire to shoot a television or film project in Israel. Even with the media reports of violence, and the current political situation, it's still a remarkably safe country, and frankly, there's nothing like being in the land of the Bible. I've personally been involved in about eight major television and film projects there, and I've found that having a production advisor "in-country" is the best and most efficient way to go.

If you have a desire to shoot a program in the Holy Land, I recommend you contact a media ministry, producer, or consultant you respect for advice on using a production manager or producer inside Israel. An experienced producer can pre-arrange everything from local crews, television and film equipment, transportation, hotels, cell phones – everything related to the production. They can also get access to locations throughout the country and help in the permitting process. I wouldn't think of shooting in Israel without an inside person paving the way.

Appendix V

Integrity in the Media:

Should a Pastor or Ministry Leader Use Ghostwriters?

—⟨∞⟩—

The rapid growth of Christian radio and television has created an era of the mega-ministry. Today, because of the impact on global audiences, large media ministries have become like international corporations, involving radio and television studios, publishing businesses, international conferences, and more.

But the bigger churches and ministries grow, the less time pastors and ministry leaders have to actually research and write books – the very products which help fund the organizations. Plus, writing well isn't easy. It's a craft and art form just like music, painting, or film-making. Writing well takes years of practice and experience, and the discipline to sit for weeks or months in front of a computer screen.

That's why sooner or later, many pastors and ministry leaders ask me about finding help to write books. Today, many pastors and ministry leaders hire professionals to do the job for them, which is a perfectly acceptable option. After all, there are many levels of working with professional writers. In my own experience, I have written for clients who gave me original material like sermon transcripts. In those cases, I was really "adapting" their own thoughts and ideas into book form. In other cases, I literally wrote it from scratch, with little more than a few interviews, a sermon tape, or a few conversations with the pastor.

But in every case, I've never received credit. In fact - in one case, I actually wrote a book for a client and then he stood up on national television and described how he had "labored night after night writing without stopping, until his wife had to beg him to get some sleep."

In another case, when a major newspaper reported that I wrote a television special for a particular media ministry, the ministry office told me to stay quiet, because they wanted people to believe that everything that came out of that ministry was written by the ministry founder.

Is this a problem? Yes and no.

No, because often writers are just happy for the work. They have certain skills, and like a professional mechanic who fixes your car, or an accountant who keeps your books, some writers are happy to do the work and get a check. They have no pressing desire to be famous, and actually enjoy writing for someone else – after all, it can pay very well.

However, a better answer is yes, because the fact is, books are far more personal than a car or a checkbook. When someone reads a book, they believe that the writing is coming from the heart of the author, and the writing style, the content, and the message reflect the name on the cover. This is true especially in the Christian world, where the message is often a spiritual message conveying eternal truth.

When a pastor or ministry leader publishes a book with only his name on it he is making a unstated promise to the reader that the material is his, coming directly from his heart and mind. He's personally presenting it in the form of this book. That's why the issue of accurate credit on the book cover is so important. If we stand for the Truth of God, then we must reflect that Truth in every area of our lives.

So is it wrong to hire a professional to help you write a book? Absolutely not. Many Christians would be shocked to see just how poorly some of our Christian leaders write, and real professionals can take an anointed message on tape from a man or woman of God and translate it into an exciting and enjoyable reading experience.

However – as a point of honor and integrity, I believe the professional writer's name should also be included on the cover along with the leader. Certainly it can be in smaller letters, or with the phrase "as written by," "edited," or "with" before the name.

Do secular authors do it? Who cares? Because we answer to a higher calling – a calling of honesty, integrity, and respect for the people God has given us to lead. Plus, I believe it's also contributed to the "celebrity" culture of Christian leaders today. They've become so well marketed, most people assume they can do anything, and do it all at the level of a superstar.

So don't hesitate to seek the help of a professional writer if you need help because of your schedule, or writing difficulties. On the other hand, don't fake it. Give the writer a little credit, and let's do our part to keep the public perception of the church to be reality and authenticity.

Appendix VI

Finding God in Hollywood

—⚊—

"Surely the Lord is in this place, and I did not know it."
— Genesis 28:16

*H*ollywood. *Tinsel town. The movie business.* For most people, those words invoke images of romance, thrills, heroism, suspense, and celebrity. On the other hand, for many *Christians* today, it generates images of illicit sex, unchecked violence, and moral depravity. I understand this more than most, because I'm a preacher's kid with a Ph.D. in Theology who has grown up in the church. But I'm *also* a working producer and director in Hollywood, so I have a ringside seat, and have to deal with both perspectives.

The movie industry is a remarkable business, and since its birth at the turn of the century has had a profound impact on the world. In 1934, in the movie "It Happened One Night", popular star Clark Gable performed without an undershirt to better display his physique and, thereafter, undershirt sales dropped dramatically. In 1942, when "Bambi" premiered, deer hunting in America dropped from a $5.7 million business to barely $1 million.

In recent years, the influence of entertainment has been even greater. A few years ago, Twentieth Century Fox Studios made an unprecedented deal with Dr. Pepper to advertise the blockbuster movie "X Men 2" on *one billion* soft drink cans.

That influence doesn't stop in the United States. International news services reported that after Afghanistan was invaded by coalition forces in the search for Osama Bin Laden, the first public buildings in that country to re-open weren't hospitals, schools, or government agencies; they were *movie theaters*, showing *American* movies.

The power of movies is significant and pervasive in this society but, as a Christian community, we have done remarkably little to harness that power for the work of the Gospel. In fact, that inability has created a strained relationship between Hollywood and the Christian community.

As a result, the church has spent far more time criticizing the movie industry than developing a positive relationship. Boycotts and public condemnation have been the typical Christian responses, but those approaches have had little impact. In fact, during the last national church driven boycott of the Walt Disney Studios, Disney's sales actually increased.

That negative approach has led the church to the creation of an entire sub-culture of *Christian* movies, most of which feature poor production values, bad acting, and sacrifice compelling storytelling for an explicit gospel presentation. While many Christians have supported films like "The Omega Code," and "Left Behind," most would agree that these films fell far short of their potential and will never be considered examples of excellent filmmaking.

But if boycotts, shame, or even creating a *Christian* movie industry doesn't make better movies, what will?

For a number of years, there have been thousands of Christians working quietly (and not so quietly) in the mainstream entertainment industry, trying to make a difference in the quality, moral values, and direction of movies and television. Sometimes, their work is obvious, such as Martha Williamson, Executive Producer of the "Touched by an Angel" television series. Some Christians have criticized Martha for not being more explicit in her episodes – especially not mentioning the name of Jesus. But week after week, Martha walked a tightrope to balance the network's demands with her Christian faith in order to reach the widest possible audience. And after all, a prime time television program that tells millions of people every week that God loves them and has a wonderful plan for their lives is not such a terrible thing.

One of the most influential and respected Christians in the movie business today is Ralph Winter, producer of films such as "The X-Men," Tim Burton's recent re-make of "The Planet of the Apes," "X2," "X3," "Fantastic Four," and some of the most successful "Star Trek" movies. He has an exclusive deal to produce major blockbuster "event" movies for Twentieth Century Fox Studios, and most of his films are budgeted in the staggering $150 million range. But at the same time Ralph has been active in fostering, encouraging, and helping Christians create smaller films that reflect spiritual values. The difference between Ralph and many other Christians who have attempted movies is that Ralph absolutely will not compromise production values or storytelling.

"People come to a movie to be entertained *first,*" he said in a recent interview. "We have to master the art of filmmaking and create a powerful story before we think about how we're going to put some kind of Christian message in the film. Most Christians fail in the film business today because even though their intentions are admirable, they haven't learned the art and skill of making a great movie. We have to earn the respect of the viewer if we're going to succeed."

Ralph's extraordinary credentials in the industry have earned him the right to be heard. His box office results have garnered billions of dollars, and many Christians in Hollywood consider him a mentor and friend. He might as well be called the "Godfather of Christians in Hollywood."

Scott Derrickson is a writer and director who is rapidly becoming one of the most sought after screenwriters and directors in the industry. He co-wrote and directed "The Exorcism of Emily Rose" and has written for the best in Hollywood, including Jerry Bruckheimer, generally considered to be the single most powerful producer in town. Like many other Christians in the entertainment industry, Scott wants to be known as both a writer and a Christian, but not as a "Christian writer."

Scott explains, "Jesus didn't tell explicitly 'Christian' stories. Many of his parables were about everyday life, and they impacted people in a powerful way. I want the movies I work on to do the same thing. When you tell a great story, people drop their defenses and give you the opportunity to share profound truth. But if they feel like you're preaching to them, they'll quickly resist and the opportunity is lost."

But the filmmaker who made big news with a faith based project was Mel Gibson with his blockbuster film "The Passion of the Christ." A Catholic believer, Mel has been one of Hollywood's highest paid actors, and his films have experienced great box office success. In recent years however, he has moved from an action movie actor to a serious filmmaker pursuing mature themes of faith, and Academy Award winning "Braveheart" established Gibson as a serious actor and director. "The Passion of the Christ" was the culmination of years of painstaking research on the last 48 hours in the life of Jesus. Gibson invested $20 to $25 million of his own money to make the movie, but despite his status as a top box office draw and Oscar winner, Hollywood's major studios shied away from distributing the film early on, due to the controversy surrounding it. Initially beset by charges of anti-Semitism and attacked by some Jewish leaders in the press, more recently, many influential leaders of both Christian and Jewish backgrounds defended the film as possibly the single greatest film on the crucifixion and resurrection of Christ ever created.

Even the Pope told his secretary after viewing the film: "It is as it was," meaning he considered it an authentic portrayal of Gospel accounts of the last hours in Christ's life. The film is based on Gospel narratives and contains dialogue only in Latin, Hebrew and Aramaic, the vernacular of ancient Palestine.

But the question remains: Are these and other Christians making a difference in Hollywood, and if so, how can we support their efforts?

While the major stories of boycotts, controversy, and condemnation sometimes make the headlines, few stories of hope ever do. And yet everyday in Hollywood, Christians experience situations that are a great encouragement to the Body of Christ.

A director on a network series said, "I don't make a big deal to my fellow workers about being a Christian, but it's amazing how people who are experiencing a divorce, or are having family or drug problems, always seem to seek me out."

One film crew member took the bold step of asking if she could pray with everyone before a big day at the studio. To her surprise, the series star stepped up and said "I've always hoped someone would say that," and the entire crew held hands and prayed.

Because of his Christian values, a writer refused a producer's request to include a violent rape scene in a script. He resigned from the show thinking his career was over. But when he got back to his office, his desk was covered in phone messages from other producers "wanting to hire someone who had the guts to stand up for what he believed."

If God chose to speak through a donkey, and if stones are capable of crying out in praise, then God certainly can work through the movie and television industry – but your help is needed.

Here's some things you can do to make a difference in Hollywood:

1) **Consider Hollywood a mission field**. We don't boycott or humiliate a tribe in another country because they don't understand Christian values, so why do it to Hollywood? Let's begin approaching Hollywood as a mission field – people who are made in the image of God, but who need to know about his loving plan for their lives.

2) **Support films with Christian values like "The Passion of the Christ," or "The Chronicles of Narnia"**. It's absolutely critical that Hollywood studios realize there is an audience for films with a Christian worldview. I would especially urge you to see these movies on their opening weekend, since that's when studios make the decision about how long the film stays in the theaters.

3) **Pray for Christians in the industry**. Every day Christians are working in an often hostile environment in a heroic effort to write, act, direct, and produce stories that celebrate faith in God. But we can't do it alone. We need the help of every Christian to provide the kind of prayer support that will open doors, soften hearts, and sometimes *make a way where there is no way*.

4) **Understand how the media can be used as a tool for evangelism.** Encourage Christian young people to pursue careers in the media, businessmen and businesswomen to fund Christian media projects, and churches to use the media in their outreaches. Movies, television, and now the Internet are the communication tools of this

culture, and if the church doesn't take them seriously, we'll lose a generation.

It doesn't take much to see that more and more, entertainment professionals are exploring themes of spirituality, redemption, and faith. The question is, is the church ready to point the way to this troubled world?

Appendix VII

An Open Letter to Christian High Schools, Colleges, and Universities

—m—

Dear Christian Educator:

I am writing to you regarding the incredible need to train young Christian men and women for careers in the media. Today, we live in a media-driven culture. George Barna's research indicates that the average home in America now has at least two television sets, and young people today spend 38 hours per week using computers, television, CDs, and other media. In fact, *by the time a typical teenager is 18 years of age, he or she has seen more than 100,000 beer commercials on television.*

In that environment, it's absolutely imperative that we train men and women as media professionals in order to counter a media-saturated, post-modern worldview that has gripped this culture.

As a media consultant to many of the largest and most successful churches in America, founding partner in a successful television commercial production company, a working producer and director in Hollywood, with a Ph.D. in Theology, I have a unique perspective on the issue. Here are the facts:

1) Today, more and more churches and ministries are using multi-media. They are heavily into broadcast television, the Internet, video projection, and other technologies in their worship services

and outreaches. The problem is finding trained Christians with the expertise to use the equipment effectively.

2) There are remarkably few organizations providing information specifically devoted to church media production and technology. To meet the growing demand for information and resources, there is significant need for Christian media professionals.

3) Media-related ministries that focus on Christians making films, television programs, DVDs, and more are some of the fastest-growing ministries in America.

4) The National Religious Broadcasters (the advocacy organization for Christian broadcasters) is experiencing record growth and impact around the world.

5) More and more Christian young people want to express themselves through the arts and media – even at middle and high-school levels.

6) Secular colleges are expanding mass communications departments, training young people to enter Hollywood and the entertainment industry with no Christian background or focus.

7) Based on my experience working with Christian colleges and universities across the country, I believe that if you expand your media programs and classes, purchase high quality equipment and facilities, and invest financially in these areas, you'll find enrollments increasing as more and more Christian young people look for ways to utilize their gifts and talents in the area of communication.

Personally, while I love to hear great gospel preaching, I've also discovered there is remarkable power in telling dramatic stories of redemption and hope. Throughout His ministry, Jesus told stories with great power and effectiveness – stories that changed people's lives. Christian colleges, universities, and seminaries have done an excellent job at training people to preach and teach, but now we are being called to train Christian filmmakers, writers, producers, and media directors to reach a new generation with new skills.

I encourage you to answer that call.

Sincerely,
Phil Cooke

Afterword

Want to Make A Difference on Television?

—ᠭᠭ—

One way every Christian can respond to what's on network television is to let the networks know your opinions. Television executives often pay attention to viewer response as an indicator of audiences' tastes and your letter can often make a significant difference. Simply write a letter to the network, and describe the specific program and how you feel about it. Remember to be gracious rather than hostile, and you'll have a far better chance of being heard.

NOTE: Network executives often change titles and companies fairly rapidly, so I'll provide the company websites here, and I would suggest you check them out for exact contact information. Generally, I recommend you write to the president of the network or the vice-president of programming.

NBC
NBC Television Network
3000 West Alameda Ave.
Burbank, CA 91523
nbc.com
Phone: (818) 840-4444

CBS
CBS Entertainment
7800 Beverly Blvd.
Los Angeles, CA 90036
cbs.com
Phone: (323) 575-2345

Disney/ABC
Walt Disney Studios
500 Circle Seven Drive
Glendale, CA 91201
disney.go.com
Phone: (818) 863-7260,
or
ABC Entertainment
500 S. Buena Vista Ave.
Burbank, CA 91521
abc.com
Phone: (818) 557-7777

FOX
Fox Entertainment
10201 W. Pico Blvd.
Los Angeles, CA 90035
fox.com
Phone: (310) 369-1000

The UPN and WB Networks (upn.com and wb.com) are making significant changes at the time of this writing, merging into a new network called the "CW" Network.

CW
CW Network
411 W. Hollywood Way
Burbank, CA 91505
cwtv.com

Also, if you see one or more specific instances where you believe a TV network is pushing "the decency envelope," you can file an informal consumer complaint with the Federal Communications Commission (FCC). There is no fee for filing such a complaint. Simply send a letter, in your own words describing the problem, to:

Federal Communications Commission
Consumer Information Bureau
Consumer Complaints
445 12th Street S.W.
Washington, D.C. 20554
Phone: 1-888-CALL-FCC or 1-888-TELL-FCC
Fax: (202) 418-0232

One of the greatest challenges the media industry faces today is a definition of indecency. As I write this chapter TV networks are asking the Federal Communications Commission to more accurately define the rules for indecency and profanity, since court rulings have made a definition rather loose and often quite random. This is a time where the influence of the Christian community needs to be felt. I would strongly urge you to personally write letters advocating stronger rules for stopping indecent behavior in the media, and encourage your church and community members to do the same.

What's Next?

—ɱ—

Your next steps in media are critical, especially if you're a pastor, ministry leader, or producer who feels you have a genuine calling to use the media as a tool for reaching this culture. But mistakes are expensive, and making the right choices can mean the difference between success and failure.

We've talked about hiring consultants, finding the right advice, thinking creatively, and assembling the best team. But as you move forward, I would encourage you to explore two important resources:

philcooke.com

My blog at philcooke.com is a daily online resource of my own thoughts, ideas, and teaching regarding faith and media. Check it out on a regular basis to learn about what's happening in Hollywood and in Christian media, what innovative believers are doing, and how you can benefit. The best way to push the envelope is to start a conversation about these difficult issues of using the media in a post-modern world. I once spoke at a media conference, and brought up some of these uncomfortable issues and afterwards, one participant said, *"I'm not really ready to go in the direction you're talking about, but as Christians, we definitely need to start this conversation."* That's what my blog is about, and I think it will stimulate your thinking, and keep you creative.

cookepictures.com

The second resource is our production and consulting company, Cooke Pictures, based in Santa Monica, California. After spending three decades working with some of the largest and most influential media ministries in the country, we've learned a few things that might help you in your particular situation. Our website is filled with teaching resources, including "free stuff" that will help you immediately, and if you need further assistance, don't hesitate to call and let us know. Our goal is to help churches and ministries raise the bar of quality and effectiveness in their media outreaches, and through individual projects or monthly consulting, we can help you pinpoint your weak spots, define your brand, and create a powerful media outreach that captures your voice and your vision.

Special Thanks

—ɯ—

I would like to thank the publishers and editors of:

Religious Broadcasting
Wireless Age
Technologies for Worship
Church Production
Vision
Millimeter
Church Business
Foursquare World Advance

For giving me a voice in religious media for more than a decade.

And especially: *Charisma* and *Ministries Today* magazines for giving me the opportunity to write monthly columns on faith and the media.